LIVING IN THE
CREATIVE
REALM

Foreword by Dr. Alveda King
LIVING IN THE CREATIVE REALM

ADVANCING THE KINGDOM THROUGH CREATIVITY

CARMELA MYLES
WITH DR. FRANCIS MYLES

Includes Prayers of Declaration & Activation

© COPYRIGHT 2022 Carmela Myles All rights reserved.

This book is protected by the copyright laws of the United States of America. This book may not be copied or reprinted for commercial gain or profit. The use of short quotations for personal or group study is permitted and encouraged. Permission will be granted upon written request.

Unless otherwise identified, Scripture quotations are from the Holy Bible, New King James Version Copyright © 1982 by Thomas Nelson, Inc. Used by permission. All rights reserved.

Scripture quotations marked KJV are also taken from the King James Version Copyright © 1982 by Thomas Nelson, Inc. Used by permission. All rights reserved.

Scripture quotations marked AMP are taken from The Amplified Bible New Testament. Copyright © 1958, 1987 by the Lockman Foundation, La Habra, California. Used by permission. The emphasis within Scripture quotations is the author's own.

Cover and Internal Design by:
Renaissance 909, a company owned by Carmela Myles
Edited by: E.D.I.T. LLC (editllc.net)
Visit the author's website at carmelamyles.com

Published by
Francis Myles International
950 Eagles Landing Parkway Unit 618
Stockbridge, GA 30281
Printed in the United States by KDP (An Amazon Company)

All rights reserved.

Library of Congress Cataloging-in-Publication Data:
An application to register this book for cataloging has been submitted to the Library of Congress.

International Standard Book Number:
Paperback ISBN: 978-1-7350513-4-5

Table of Contents

Acknowledgements 7
Foreward 9
Preface 13

1. Calling Those Things That Be Not! 19
2. The Spirit of Creativity 26
3. Communion with the Spirit of Creativity 42
4. The Book of Destiny – Our Divine Design 54
5. Our God-Given Divine Potential 67
6. Our Innate Wisdom 77
7. You are God's Masterpiece; a Walking Piece of Art ... 92
8. Detox your Mind! 101
9. Fear Not! 121
10. How are you Spending your Time? 129
11. How to Activate your Creativity 144
12. The Power to Create Wealth Through Creativity 160
13. Creativity and Personality 172
14. My Creative Journey 188

Endnotes 201

ACKNOWLEDGEMENTS

> The Lord gave the word: great was the company of those that published it"
>
> *(Psalm 68:11 KJV).*

WHAT WE BECOME IN GOD is a sum total of the divine encounters we have had, the people we have met, our personal experiences and the books we have read. The saying "No man is an island" is certainly true in the context of authoring this book. I want to acknowledge the impact that the following men and women of God have had on my life:

My husband Francis Myles has continually encouraged me to be the person God created me to be. He has imparted so much wisdom in me. I have been impacted by the books he has written that contain revelation required for living victoriously in my lifetime. I have grown so much in the things of God since I married him. I respect and honor him. He is the love of my life. I love you honey!

My father Romeo Real is now with the Lord. He taught me to persevere regardless of my situation. He came to know the Lord before he passed away in 2003. During his last days he became so thankful and appreciative of the beauty of His creation. I remember him stopping his car at the Palisades Parkway in NJ. He stepped out of his car gasping in awe by the beauty of the trees changing colors during that fall season. I love you dad and I miss you. Thank you for all you've done to make sure that we are always taken care of.

My mother Avelina Real has been a pillar for me. She is my greatest intercessor and prayer warrior. She has never ceased praying for her children. I know that my life has turned out the way it is because of her fervent prayers for me. She is an epitome of a quiet and gentle giant. I love you mom.

To my brothers, Romeo III, Ronald, Randy and Robin, my sister, Anna Marie and my niece Katrina: I love, honor and celebrate you. I believe in the creativity God have given you!

To Linda Vega and Karen Hosey: you both have shown me your love and genuine heart to see me succeed. Your wisdom and counsel have been impeccable. Most important, you have never given up on me! I love you both!

To all our family and friends who have always encouraged me, there is no jealousy in their hearts toward my husband and me, but only their love and desire to see the Kingdom of God manifest through us. I am forever grateful to all of you. I honor and celebrate you and I love you more than you know.

To all our destiny helpers: I am very grateful for the time and energy that you have spent to help us in our journey. We could have not done it without you. I salute you and I honor and celebrate all of you. May the seed of time, energy and hard work you have sown in our life tremendously multiply in your lives.

Special thanks to my friend Daina Doucet. We have come a long way. Thank you for taking me under your wings when I lived in Canada and thank you for helping me take this book into another level.

While the material in this book is original, there are a few quotes throughout that have been taken from the published works of other authors to add depth to the topic or focus. Each is documented in the "Endnotes Section."

Foreword

Carmela Myles' book, *Living In The Creative Realm*, is truly a living, breathing testimony. Remarkably, the book is not just a testimony, but also a how-to guide to recognizing, activating, and using our God-given creativity to advance God's Kingdom in the earth.

As a prophetic creative being, Carmela is living proof that we as human beings are created in the image and likeness of God. As a result, as members of the "one blood human race," with God's help, we can actually dream, envision, act and create success for advancing the Kingdom of God.

> ...and hath made of one blood all nations of men for to dwell on all the face of the earth, and hath determined the times before appointed, and the bounds of their habitation; that they should seek the Lord, if haply they might feel after him, and find him, though he be not far from every one of us: for in him we live, and move, and have our being; as certain also of your own poets have said, For we are also his offspring.
>
> *(Acts 17:26-28 KJV)*

Carmela blesses us, the readers, with her book. Because she has the added advantage of being half of a powerful Kingdom building duo, her punch has more power. Together, Dr. Francis Myles and creative Carmela Myles are Kingdom leaders with tremendous authority as believers.

> Again I say unto you, that if two of you shall agree on earth as touching anything that they shall ask, it shall be done for them of my Father which is in heaven.
>
> *(Matthew 18:19 KJV)*

There is tremendous generosity in their creativity; their willingness to add to and support others is amazing. A good example is Carmela's response to a request for a new painting while finishing her book. Rather than saying she was too busy and pushing the request aside, she opened her heart to the prompting of the Holy Spirit, and her new painting "The Eighth Mountain" was born while finishing this book. God's creativity is not bound.

During his lifetime, Dr. Myles Munroe often mentioned the graveyard full of unfulfilled dreams; creative offerings aborted, or unborn. The questions remain:

What other products or inventions haven't been manifested on earth yet?

Who are they assigned to, and can these people manifest their dreams and visions from the creative realm into the natural realm?

Are you one of the frozen chosen?

As Carmela's sister "creative activator" in Christ, I'm honored to contribute this foreword. I must admit that while reading Carmela's book, the fires of my creativity are being fanned into higher heights and deeper depths. I'm "re-fired" in areas I had almost considered "retired."

Foreward

One of the offerings Carmela has released is the concept of having Holy Ghost "play dates" and being "a playmate with God." Wow, and Wow! While I've often envisioned Jesus, the Living Word, creating (especially when I read Colossians) with God's grace, Carmela is bringing the God Creative Relationship to greater heights and deeper depths.

I won't try to rewrite the book; Carmela's testimony and how-to approach are already remarkable. Instead, with gratitude and thanksgiving to God for this book and the author, let me share this as I close:

Ask a little child, "What do you want to be when you grow up?" Because they are young and not yet beset by the cares of the world, they are often unaware of what human eyes and ears haven't seen. They are unaware of the many facets of treasures God has seeded into them that they will carry all their lives. If these seeds are watered, they will grow. If not…

As a little girl, even before I gave my life to Christ, I was "a creative," even though I didn't understand what that meant. My parents, grandparents, aunt, and uncle considered me enigmatic, but they loved me, so they indulged what they considered to be my fancies and fantasies. Looking back, I now realize they were closet creatives too. After all, like my Uncle MLK (Dr. Martin Luther King), we all, too, had a dream.

Growing up, as a student, with fascination, I embraced studies of the historical Renaissance Period, a global season of enlightenment where human creativity abounded. Somehow, during those years, I instinctively resisted the efforts of others to bridle the flow of creativity in my veins.

As a result, by God's grace, today, as a "bondservant of Christ, I'm a "Creative Christian Evangelist." It is my honor to salute my sister in Christ, Carmela Myles, for having the compassion, love, and courage to write this book. Get ready! You are about to soar as you turn every page. God bless you.

Alveda C. King, PhD

Alveda C. King, PhD is the daughter of the late slain civil rights activist Rev. A. D. King and the niece of Dr. Martin Luther King, Jr., and a Christian Evangelist. Author of the best seller KING RULES and WE'RE NOT COLORBLIND, she is also founder of Speak for Life, Chairman of the Center for The American Dream -AFPI, and currently serves as a Fox News Channel contributor and is the host of "Alveda King's House" on Fox Nation and NEWSMAX opinion contributor; a member of Optimist International; former college professor; and a film and music veteran. Alveda is also a former Georgia State Legislator, college professor, a twice assigned Presidential appointee, and a 2021 recipient of the Presidential Lifetime Achievement Award.

PREFACE

In the beginning, God created the heavens and the earth.

(Genesis 1:1)

Creativity is seeing something that doesn't exist already. You need to find out how you can bring it into being, and that way be a playmate with God.

(Michele Shea)

I have finally written this book after numerous requests and encouragement from my dear and precious husband, Francis Myles. I told God I am only writing it if it will glorify Him and activate His children to discover what He has already deposited in them. I believe what Francis said, "If something God put in His people is activated, they will change."

In my travels to different nations, I find that most people struggle to make ends meet. Some are highly frustrated because they have not discovered the many facets of treasures God has put in them, ones they have been carrying all their lives. God has burdened me to see His children uncover these treasures. I desire anyone who comes across this book to experience a rebirth in their creativity and be inspired to ignite their passion to create.

Living in the Creative Realm

Someone once said, "We were born creative and grow up uncreative!" I certainly refuse to be a statistic of this statement. I always believe that destiny is by choice, not by chance. We are constantly presented with choices. I pray we make destiny choices that extend His Kingdom. Creativity can be learned, so we can choose to spend a good percentage of our time being creative.

I also pray that this book will inspire everyone who reads it. No matter where they are in their creative walk, may they create, create again, or create more. Being creative is in the heart of God. The first verb or action word in the Bible was the word created, as stated in Genesis 1:1, *"In the beginning, God created the heavens and the earth."* I sincerely pray that this book will inspire everyone who reads it, regardless of where they are in their creative walk, to choose to be described as being creative.

We will find that two types of creating are used interchangeably in the Bible. The Hebrew word *bara* is typically used when God is creating something out of nothing – things that do not exist on earth – so they can only come from the spiritual realm.

The Hebrew word *asah* is typically used for creating something out of something that exists.

God has filled the heavens and the earth with everything we need to be creative. Some of our clothes are made out of cotton; leather shoes are made of animal skins; cars are made out of steel, which is an alloy made of iron; alcohol is produced by the fermentation of sugars by yeasts, and tires are made of natural rubber that comes from the milky white sap of rubber trees. The list goes on and on; we hopefully get the gist of it! The questions are,

What are other products or inventions that haven't been manifested on earth yet?

Who are they assigned to, and can these people manifest them from the creative realm into the natural realm?

PREFACE

Are you one of these people?

What is creativity?

According to *Lexico.com,* creativity is "the use of imagination or original ideas, especially in the production of an artistic work." *Encyclopedia Britannica* defines it as "the ability to make or otherwise bring into existence something new, whether a new solution to a problem, a new method or device, or a new artistic object or form."

Based on my Holy Spirit-inspired definition, creativity is the ability to discover and connect with our God-given design, creative potential, and divine wisdom through communion with the Holy Spirit, who is the Spirit of Creativity. This book is based on the definition He gave me. I will expand its definition in Chapters 2 to 6.

The difference between creativity and innovation

Creativity occurs when people use their imaginations to create new ideas, solve problems and think of possibilities that no one else has thought of before. The scope of creativity is limited only by one's ability to think outside the norm. The nature of creativity means that an idea's creation is unique and original to the creative thinker. Creativity is not a genetic trait, but something a person develops as they continue to learn and grow and use their imagination for various forms of expression. Creativity has no inherent value unless a person manifests it into reality.

You will learn, as you continue to read this book, that creativity is learned and developed as we purpose in our hearts and minds to develop its "muscles." The world can say whatever they want, but creativity can only be harnessed by accessing divine inspirations in communion with the Holy Spirit, who can access everything in God's heart. I therefore pray that this book will take you to the place of accessing the Mind of God for the release of new ideas and concepts that become a solution in our world.

Innovation is the process of exploiting the benefit of creative ideas for commercial and financial success. Innovation is the creation of an innovator. Since innovation is the application of creative ideas, it's innately connected to creativity. They work in tandem with one another. Innovation can be a physical object, a concept to improve, or the creation of a new process. People innovate to solve a problem, or make society functionally more convenient.[1]

The world is constantly changing, and as believers, we cannot fall behind in creativity and innovation. Many products and businesses have become dinosaurs because of rapid changes in technology and how we live and conduct business. Old technologies like the typewriter, floppy disks, VCR, Polaroid cameras, old chunky telephones, and the Walkman by Sony that changed how we listen to music, are now obsolete. They have been replaced by superior technological advancements that are faster and more efficient. Who would have thought that we can now borrow movies digitally through Netflix and Amazon Prime making Blockbuster video obsolete?

Our phones have now become our portable pocket office managers on which we can conduct our banking, learning and education, and accounting. They are portable TVs and radios! Who would have thought? And I guarantee that in ten years, some of the companies we know now will not exist because of future technologies that will be invented. If we, therefore, don't purpose in our minds to become more creative and access the mind of God through the power of the Holy Spirit, we will not be able to produce the products of the future. I genuinely hope this book can activate and give us the inspiration to start living in the creative realm.

Living in the creative realm

It is a big fat lie to believe we are not creative. I bet if I asked a group of people if they are creative, more than half would not raise their hands. I have good news for those who do not believe in the creativity that lies in the depth of their being:

Preface

Everyone can create!

We are always creating something. We create the moment we dress in the morning – we choose the color of a blouse or shirt to match the pair of pants we want to wear that day, and add the right pair of shoes to complete our chosen outfit. I have seen women dressed beautifully with everything matching: bags, shoes, earrings, watch, bracelets! By the time they leave their house, they are a walking piece of art based on the clothes and accessories they have chosen to wear that day.

Similarly, when we cook meat, fish, vegetables, starches, and add salads, our table becomes a finished canvas together with our plates, utensils and the food arrangements on the table. How many times have we eaten in restaurants where we have taken pictures of the meal because of how beautifully the chef arranged it on our plate? In some Asian restaurants we can find a flower on our dish made of peeled carrots, or a radish beautifully carved to garnish our food.

Every day we are creating something!

Creativity is activated in ways you will not consider creative. It comes in our day-to-day living. It happens when we wake up hungry and without a recipe cook together ingredients we have found in our kitchen.

Tailors create outfits by repurposing old clothes into an innovative design.

Drummers produce sounds that make you dance and feel good using pots, pans, plastic containers, spoons and forks.

Choreographers use various props to produce visual arts through dance.

Photographers shoot at the most obscure angle and come up with an award-winning photo.

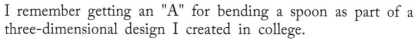

I remember getting an "A" for bending a spoon as part of a three-dimensional design I created in college.

Creativity can be endless and limitless. It is only limited by our minds.

It all started in the garden

When I was a new believer, the Lord gave me a vision. I was in prayer, and suddenly I was in the Garden of Eden! It was sunny and peaceful. Then the atmosphere changed, and it became dark. An eerie feeling engulfed me as I lost my peace. By the spirit, I knew it was the moment that Adam and Eve ate the fruit of the Tree of the Knowledge of Good and Evil, and somehow, I felt God's emotion and sadness. I heard in my spirit, *All I want is to continue to create with them.* God loves to create. I can just imagine how elated and joyful He was when He created the animals and allowed Adam to name them. Adam was part of His creativity.

How can He possibly not do the same thing with us?

We were created by a creative God. There is no way His creativity is not flowing through us. According to Genesis 2:7, *"And the Lord God formed man of the dust of the ground, and breathed into his nostrils the breath of life; and man became a living being."* When He breathed on us, He did not just breathe air into man; He breathed the Breath of Life, the *Ruach* who is His Spirit and the Spirit of Creativity, whom Jesus also imparted to His disciples. Jesus said to them again, *"Peace to you! As the Father has sent Me, I also send you.' And when He had said this, He breathed on them, and said to them, 'Receive the Holy Spirit'"* (John 20:21-22). It is my prayer that this book will open your eyes to the realm of creativity where Kingdom ideas are waiting to be discovered!

In His Love,
Carmela Myles

CHAPTER 1

CALLING THOSE THINGS THAT BE NOT!

By Dr. Francis Myles

I have contributed to other people's books, but none has pleased me as much as contributing one chapter to my wife's new book, *Living in the Creative Realm*. Many of you will better appreciate my excitement when you understand the origins of this book.

I have been encouraging my wife to write a book for the longest. She hesitated because she was not sure what she should write. Then one day we were in the car on one of our Africa ministry trips when the Spirit of God came upon me. I prophesied to my wife, "You need to write a book called *Living in the Creative Ream*." There was something about the title that resonated within her spirit. I saw a flash of excitement and inspiration through her eyes for the first time.

It was easy for me to prophesy this because my wife is one of the most creative people I know. Her prophetic paintings, born out of the creative realm she lives in, decorate the altar at most of our conferences. Many of our ministry partners and followers have my wife's paintings hanging in their homes or offices. In one instance, a partner of our ministry gave her testimony to an auditorium full of people at our KINGS 2021 conference. She shared that one of her brothers woke up from a coma in a hospital when she wrapped him in one of my wife's prophetic blankets.

That is proof that anything created by God that proceeds from the creative realm, can carry the anointing or presence of God.

> As it is written, "I have made you a father of many nations" in the presence of Him whom he believed—God, who gives life to the dead and calls those things which do not exist as though they did.
>
> *(Romans 4:17)*

Few Scriptures capture the driving spiritual technology behind operating in the creative realm of God's Kingdom, like Romans 4:17. We will see why when we break down the Scripture.

The verse begins with the words "as it is written," implying that Kingdom creativity is born out of tapping into the mind of the Holy Spirit to project what is already written in heaven here on earth. This passage means that there is a lot in the invisible and yet very tangible Kingdom of Heaven that needs to manifest here on earth to better, or brighten the lives of men with God's limitless resources. I am convinced from watching my wife that one of the ways God uses to manifest His Kingdom here on earth is through the Spirit of Creativity operating under His influence in yielded vessels like my wife. I gasp at God's endless beauty whenever, under the inspiration of the Holy Spirit, she creates another breathtaking painting, scarf, or blanket. I find myself saying, "There is no way that came from her head without divine inspiration."

The second part of Romans 4:17 says, *"I have made you a father of many nations."* This shows us that anytime we start to tap into what's "written in heaven," God begins to make us into the person we were ordained to become in relation to what is already written about us in our Book of Destiny. I have watched as my wife's creative grace has super-abounded whenever she yielded herself, again and again, to the Holy Spirit's creative flow through her.

May you become the creative person God ordained you to be!

Calling Those Things That Be Not!

My wife and I are convinced that creativity is resident in some form or fashion in each human being created by a creative God!

The third part of Romans 4:17 says, "...*in the presence of Him.*" This statement really excites me! It makes clear that God's presence is the only spiritual atmosphere anyone needs for being creative. I am convinced that God's presence is saturated with every form of creativity you can imagine.

My wife will take you deeper into the height, width, and depth of the Spirit of Creativity. You will come to appreciate that you don't have to be an artist of paintings, or a clothing designer like my wife, to be creative. You can be creative in any Kingdom assignment with which the Lord has mantled you. The reason many of God's people are not creative is primarily two-fold:

- First, they do not spend any meaningful time in the presence of God. Their lives are too busy (so they think) to spend quality time in the presence of the Creator. No doubt their supposed "busyness" is due to satan's trickery. He doesn't want them to access God's limitless resources, resident in His manifest presence.

- Second, most believers miss participating in the creative realm because they have convinced themselves that they are not creative. This, too, is a lie of the enemy of our soul, because God gave man His creative spirit in Genesis 1:26. Said simply, we are all creative at some level because we carry the DNA of a creative God, for we are the sheep of His pasture.

The fourth phrase in Romans 4:17 says, "*Him whom he believed!*" This verse shows us that the Spirit of Creativity does not circumvent one of the most fundamental laws of the Kingdom, e.g., the law of faith (see Hebrews 11:6). Faith is one of the essential spiritual currencies of the Kingdom of God. Without faith, it is impossible to please, or access the limitless resources of the Kingdom of God. God requires faith from anyone who wants to be used by Him. To acquire a creative solution to a problem, or become the creative person God has ordained you to be, you must approach Him in faith. In Abraham's case, believing God transformed him into a father of many nations. I wonder what He will make of you, or do for you in the "creative space" if you dare to approach Him in believing faith?

The fifth phrase in Romans 4:17 says, "*God, who gives life to the dead.*" This statement leads us right into the power source behind all Kingdom creativity. God is the source and power behind all forms of creativity because everything is dead on arrival without Him. Only God can bring life and creativity out of death. That is why the world is filled with people full of ideas that never amount to anything. They lack the divine inspiration (breath) to take them from death to life!

I pray that God will breathe on the creative aspects of your brain so they can begin to function at maximum capacity.

The final and sixth phrase in Romans 4:17 that I want to draw your attention to is, "*...and calls those things which do not exist as though they did.*" This statement captures the essence and premise behind all Kingdom creativity. The premise behind all Kingdom creativity is the art of "*calling those things which do not exist as though they did.*" It is *manifesting the invisible attributes of God in the visible realm.* This aspect of creativity endears the spirit of faith because faith, by its definitive nature, as stated in Hebrews 11:1, has to do with manifesting the unseen into the seen realm of men.

As you read this book, I pray that your faith will be stirred up to operate in realms of creativity you have never known before.

Prayer of Release #1
– Calling Those Things that Be Not!

Supernatural Decrees for Breakthrough

The Word says in Job 22:28, "decree a thing and it shall be established," therefore,

- I decree and declare that the creativity I have exists in the mind of God, who is in heaven, and manifests in my life here on earth.

- I decree and declare that I have the faith to appropriate the creativity of the Kingdom by *"calling those things which do not exist as though they did."* Through my creativity, I manifest the invisible attributes of God in the visible realm.

- I decree and declare that I am a yielded vessel of creativity. God's endless beauty under the inspiration of the Holy Spirit creates through me.

- I decree and declare that God is breathing on the creative aspects of my brain so I can function at the maximum capacity of my creativity.

- I acknowledge that without faith it is impossible to access the limitless resources of the Kingdom of God. I decree and declare supernatural faith over my life for the advancement of His Kingdom through me.

- I decree and declare that because I approach God in faith, He graces me to be the creative solution.

LIFE APPLICATION SECTION

Memory Verse

As it is written, "I have made you a father of many nations" in the presence of Him whom he believed — God, who gives life to the dead and calls those things which do not exist as though they did. *(Romans 4:17)*

Reflections

1. What is the connection between calling things that be not as though they are and the Spirit of Creativity?

   _____
   _____
   _____
   _____
   _____

2. According to Romans 4:17, how did God make Abraham the father of many nations?

   _____
   _____
   _____
   _____
   _____

CHAPTER 2

THE SPIRIT OF CREATIVITY

> Creativity is the ability to discover and connect with our God-given design, creative potential, and divine wisdom through communion with the Holy Spirit, who is the Spirit of Creativity.
>
> *(Carmela Myles)*

> You send forth Your Spirit, they are created; And You renew the face of the earth.
>
> *(Psalm 104:30)*

> Creative thinking inspires ideas, and these ideas inspire change.
>
> *(Barbara Januszkiewicz)*

When God created man, He breathed into his nostrils the breath of life: *"Then the Lord God formed a man from the dust of the ground and breathed into his nostrils the breath of life, and the man became a living being"*(Genesis 2:7). He breathed the breath of life on man's lifeless body of dust. Man was given a substance not created on earth to give him life. The breath of God is the Holy Spirit! In John 20:21-22, we read, *"So Jesus said to them again, 'Peace to you! As the Father sent Me, I also send you.' And when He said this, He breathed on them, 'Receive the Holy Spirit.'* When Jesus breathed on His disciples, they all received the Holy Spirit. He is God's creative power and the One responsible for imparting it. The Holy Spirit is the Spirit of Creativity.

> In the beginning, God created the heavens and the earth. The earth was without form, and void; and darkness was on the face of the deep. And the Spirit of God was hovering over the face of the waters. Then God said, "Let there be light;" and there was light. And God saw the light, that it was good; and God divided the light from the darkness.
>
> *(Genesis 1:1-4)*

Notice that in this part of the Scripture Moses talked about God creating the heavens and the earth. However, at the time of creation, the earth was without form; it was void, and darkness was at hand, meaning there was confusion, emptiness, and obscurity. Then He introduced the Spirit of God hovering over the face of the waters. The Law of First Mention emphasizes the importance of the first time a word is mentioned in the Bible, primarily found in the book of Genesis. According to *GrowinginJesus.com*, "the law of first mention is the principle in the interpretation of Scripture which states that the first mention or occurrence of a subject in Scripture establishes an unchangeable pattern, with that subject remaining unchanged in the Mind of God throughout the Scripture."

The Holy Spirit was first mentioned hovering over the face of the waters right after the writer described the earth as being without form, void, and dark. Wow! Hovering means to brood, or fertilize, to move gently, and relax. Brooding is when a hen sits on her eggs to incubate them and makes them warm in preparation for hatching. Another wow!

The Holy Spirit is our incubator. He prepares us to be hatched into our purpose and destiny; He is the One that gives us light when we are in darkness. He hovers over us to fill the voids in our lives and free us from the confusion and darkness in which we find ourselves. God transforms us back into the original form He has made us to be! Therefore, He is also the One who activates God's creativity trapped within us!

Who is Bezalel?

According to Exodus 25:8-9, God said, *"And let them make Me a sanctuary, that I may dwell among them. According to all that I show you, that is, the pattern of the tabernacle and the pattern of all its furnishings, just so you shall make it."* God specifically instructed Moses to build Him a sanctuary – a dwelling place so that He could dwell among the people. He was precise and detailed in the pattern, design, type of material, and colors of the place where He was to dwell. Most important, God told Moses He would show the artists the pattern so they could make it exactly like what was on His mind!

Bezalel was the solution to fulfilling God's specific purpose of building Him a tabernacle. Exodus 31:1-4 tells us,

> Then the Lord spoke to Moses, saying: "See, I have called by name Bezalel the son of Uri, the son of Hur, of the tribe of Judah. And I have filled him with the Spirit of God, in wisdom, in understanding, in knowledge, and in all manner of workmanship, to design artistic works, to work in gold, in silver, in bronze, in cutting jewels for setting, in carving wood, and to work in all manner of workmanship.

God called Bezalel a craftsman and filled him with the Spirit of God. Thus, the first time we see a man filled by the Spirit of God, the emphasis was not on whether he was a king, or a priest, or whether his office was of an apostle, prophet, pastor, teacher, or evangelist, but it was on his creativity. He was a master workman, or craftsman under Moses, the son of Uri, son of Hur, of the tribe of Judah. God gave him special wisdom and skills for his task. Then God provided and appointed destiny helpers,

Aholiab and Ahisamach, to assist him with the task. Not only that, God put wisdom in the hearts of all the gifted artisans so they could make all that God commanded them to do, from the Tabernacle of Meeting, to the priestly garments as described in Exodus 31:6-10 below:

> And I, indeed I, have appointed with him Aholiab the son of Ahisamach, of the tribe of Dan; and I have put wisdom in the hearts of all the gifted artisans, that they may make all that I have commanded you: the tabernacle of meeting, the ark of the Testimony and the mercy seat that is on it, and all the furniture of the tabernacle – the table and its utensils, the pure gold lampstand with all its utensils, the altar of incense, the altar of burnt offering with all its utensils, and the laver and its base – the garments of ministry, the holy garments for Aaron the priest and the garments of his sons, to minister as priests, and the anointing oil and sweet incense for the holy place. According to all that I have commanded you they shall do.

God's stages of creating something out of something that already exists

In Chapter 5, I will explain the stages of creating out of nothing.

In this section we will explore Exodus 25:8-9 and Exodus 31:1-10, where we find the different stages of creating from something that already exists.

I pray we will find these stages helpful in giving us guidance and understanding as we embark on our creative journey.

1. **God gives us the instruction on what to create.**
   Exodus 25:8 states, *"And let them make Me a sanctuary."* Moses was instructed to make a sanctuary. We never have to worry about being left in the dark when it comes to creating,

since God always gives instructions for what He wants to build. The question is,

What is God instructing you to do, or create?

2. He gives us the purpose of why we have to make it.

Exodus 25:8 states, "*...that I may dwell among them.*" The purpose of the sanctuary was for God to be able to dwell among His people. Whatever God has instructed you to create, He will give you the purpose of why He wants you to do it. Myles Munroe used to say, "If you don't know the purpose of a thing, abuse is inevitable."

3. He promises to give us the pattern and show us how to make it.

Exodus 25:9 states, "*According to all that I show you, that is, the pattern of the tabernacle and the pattern of all its furnishings, just so you shall make it.*"

This stage is very exciting! God will never instruct us to make or create something without showing us the pattern. The phrase "will show" is from the Hebrew word, *mareh*, meaning to perceive, see, be visible, learn about, observe and watch. And "pattern" is from the Hebrew word *tabnit*, which means design, plan, construction, form, and figure. Therefore, whenever God instructs us to create something, He first opens our spiritual eyes to see the pattern, or design of what He wants us to create. He then gives us the wisdom to plan, the grace to learn about it, and the knowledge to construct His design!

4. He called him (Bezalel) by his name.

Exodus 31:1-2 states, "*Then the Lord spoke to Moses, saying: "See, I have called by name Bezalel the son of Uri, the son of Hur, of the tribe of Judah."*" God knows our name, lineage, and where we came from, and He has already chosen us to do or make something to advance His Kingdom. Bezalel was called by his name. A proclamation, an official announcement, or declaration was made public about his assignment. That led me to believe there is already an official proclamation and declaration about what we must do. We must discover it.

You probably know what you are to do. You just need to be activated to finally get it done. The question is,

What did God call you to do or create?

5. **He filled him with the Spirit of God in wisdom, understanding, knowledge, and all kinds of workmanship or craftsmanship.**

    In Exodus 31:3-5, we find what we were filled with,

    > And I have filled him with the Spirit of God, in wisdom, in understanding, in knowledge, and in all manner of workmanship, to design artistic works, to work in gold, in silver, in bronze, in cutting jewels for setting, in carving wood, and to work in all manner of workmanship.

    a. Wisdom – the ability to have good judgment and discernment.
    b. Understanding – the fact or condition of knowing something with familiarity gained through experience or association and having comprehension.
    c. Knowledge – skills acquired by a person through experience or education; the theoretical or practical understanding of a subject.
    d. All manner of workmanship – the art or skill of a craftsperson. God gave them the skills "*...to design artistic works, to work in gold, in silver, in bronze, in cutting jewels for setting, in carving wood, and to work in all manner of workmanship*" (Exodus 31:4-5).

This stage is very liberating! It shows us that we should not be blinded, and that we are never alone in creating. We have the guidance of the Spirit of the living God, the Spirit of Creativity, to do it. Bezalel was filled with the Spirit of God. He gives us the wisdom to create, the knowledge, understanding, and the skills to do it. Hence, there should never be an excuse not to manifest what He has given us to do.

6. **He appointed destiny helpers who are gifted artisans to assist him in fulfilling his assignment.**

Exodus 31:6, *"And I, indeed I, have appointed with him Aholiab the son of Ahisamach, of the tribe of Dan."* In this Scripture, we see that Bezalel has nothing to do with the appointment of the one assisting him. God appointed Aholiab to work with him. The word "appointed" is from the Hebrew word, *natati*, which means consecrate, have selected, devote and dedicate.

It is important to discern those appointed by God to assist us. How often have we hired people in our organizations and businesses who were not appointed and consecrated by God? We are related, or we are friends with them, or even better, we hired them because they are very nice believers from the church, and it turned out to be the most disastrous decision we ever made. Even if they continuously failed to perform, Donald Trump's "You're fired!" seems to be removed from our vocabulary. Unsanctified mercy kicks in so we forget our true assignment for His Kingdom.

Aholiab was specifically dedicated, consecrated, or set apart by God to assist Bezalel to pioneer God's project. I believe one of the keys we often miss in fulfilling our assignment is to recognize our destiny helpers. Ruth needed Naomi to meet Boaz; Isaac married his wife, Rebekah, because of Abraham's faithful servant who traveled a long way to find her.

In our quest to fulfill our assignments from God to create, we should rest assured that men and women are already prepared and appointed to help us.

The importance of recognizing our destiny helpers cannot be understated.

Four types of destiny helpers:

1. *Divine Connectors* – These are destiny helpers who don't hesitate to connect people because they can see through their spiritual eyes the giftings and assignments that need to merge for the advancement of the Kingdom. True destiny helpers are not hindered by jealousy or hidden agendas and welcome the opportunity to connect people. Their primary purpose is for the advancement of the Kingdom. We find an example of a divine connector in the story of Naaman. He was healed because of a recommendation made by an unknown young girl who waited on his wife.

   In 2 Kings 5:1-3 it says:

   > Now Naaman, commander of the army of the king of Syria, was a great and honorable man in the eyes of his master, because by him the Lord had given victory to Syria. He was also a mighty man of valor, but a leper. And the Syrians had gone out on raids, and had brought back captive a young girl from the land of Israel. She waited on Naaman's wife. Then she said to her mistress, "If only my master were with the prophet who is in Samaria! For he would heal him of his leprosy."

When we read the rest of 2 Kings 5, we find that Naaman was indeed healed through the ministry of Elisha, the prophet in Samaria. I advise us never to stereotype, or put divine connectors in a box, because they could be any person we meet every day, like the unknown young girl captured from the land of Israel.

2. *Men of Influence* – These are men of power and authority over their spheres of influence. They know how to dominate and have dominion over what God has given them. They know how to occupy and inhabit the territory God has assigned them. These are government officials, CEOs, church leaders, and those who can gather followers, change cultures and transform nations.

3. *Gifted People* – People gifted in different areas of business, ministry, and personal life are sent by God to help.

    We have been blessed with a strong media team from the Philippines. I am still in awe of how God put us together. I met Jeriel, who happened to be from the Philippines, through the internet while looking for someone to work on our website. They have always gone the extra mile to help our ministry grow.

    Jeriel is very gifted in this area, and eight years later, his team has been integral in our ministry in helping us with our websites, social media, and other related areas.

4. *Burden Bearers* – These are divine helpers with no hidden agendas. They are the ones who pray for us – whose shoulders have been dedicated to carrying our burdens. They are there during the best seasons of our lives, and they don't leave during our dry seasons. They are not influenced by our destiny killers and robbers. They weather our faults

and weaknesses and don't abandon us. Instead, they have a passion for bringing out the best in us. They also don't harbor offense. They brush it off and continue carrying our burdens.

We have been blessed with burden bearers whose names will never be mentioned here. They are not comfortable with being mentioned, because their assignment is not about making names for themselves. That is one of the essential qualities of burden bearers – they don't have to be known and they don't seek recognition. They know deep in their hearts they are called to us because God was the one who put the burden on them. They don't worry about being known, because they understand that whatever they do is recorded in heaven, and that's all that matters.

Who are your destiny helpers?

I decree and declare that His wisdom is upon you to recognize and discern them as they come your way!

7. He put wisdom in the hearts of all the gifted artisans so they could help him make all they were commanded to do.

Exodus 31:6 states, *"And I, indeed I, have appointed with him Aholiab the son of Ahisamach, of the tribe of Dan; and I have put wisdom in the hearts of all the gifted artisans, that they may make all that I have commanded you."*

Another liberating kingdom principle!

Our destiny helpers are commanded to help us; they were charged and ordered to stand with us. It can't get any better than that. However, some refuse to allow destiny helpers to assist them. God sends them, and they reject them. That is a critical component.

I've seen it time and time again. I have met many believers who are overwhelmed because they have not gotten the revelation that there are people commanded and charged to help them. In addition, these people are already equipped with wisdom in their hearts. They are gifted with skills and have their instructions on what they need to do to help us fulfill the assignment God has given us.

It is my prayer for you dear reader, to discover the destiny helpers already assigned to help you.

Never worry about provision for your creativity

Now that I have expounded on the stages of creating something out of something that already exists, I pray that we never worry about how our creative ideas will be funded. This should be the last thing we should worry about. If you find yourself struggling with thoughts about funding, I want to ease your mind by taking you to the beginning of Exodus Chapter 25.

> Then the Lord spoke to Moses, saying: "Speak to the children of Israel, that they bring Me an offering. From everyone who gives it willingly with his heart you shall take My offering. And this *is* the offering which you shall take from them: gold, silver, and bronze; blue, purple, and scarlet *thread,* fine linen, and goats' *hair;* ram skins dyed red, badger skins, and acacia wood; oil for the light, and spices for the anointing oil and for the sweet incense; onyx stones, and stones to be set in the ephod and in the breastplate.
>
> *(Exodus 25:1-7)*

In this passage we find the Lord telling Moses to ask the children of Israel to bring Him an offering. He was very specific, insisting it be taken only from those who had willingness in their hearts to give. He was also very specific about the type of offering to be taken. He wanted gold, silver, acacia wood and stones for setting into the ephod and in the breastplate of the priests.

This is very clear and simple to me. The Lord has already put in the hearts of those who are willing everything we need in order to finish the creative projects He assigns.

Wow! He has already asked the willing vessels to give Him the specific things we need as an offering. When my spiritual eyes were opened to this revelation, I got so excited! I realized my projects were already financed before He even asked me to do them.

I pray that you receive this revelation as well. You never have to worry about where the money to finish your God-given creative ideas comes from!

The call to teach and multiply

In Exodus 31, we learned about the call of Bezalel as a gifted artisan and master craftsman whose primary assignment was to build a dwelling place for the Lord. Another aspect of his calling is introduced in Exodus 35:

> And Moses said to the children of Israel, "See, the Lord has called by name Bezalel the son of Uri, the son of Hur, of the tribe of Judah; and He has filled him with the Spirit of God, in wisdom and understanding, in knowledge and all manner of workmanship, to design artistic works, to work in gold and silver and bronze, in cutting jewels for setting, in carving wood, and to work in all manner of artistic workmanship.
>
> And He has put in his heart the ability to teach, in him and Aholiab the son of Ahisamach, of the tribe of Dan. He has filled them with skill to do all manner of work of the engraver and the designer and the tapestry maker, in blue, purple, and

> scarlet thread, and fine linen, and of the weaver—those who do every work and those who design artistic works.
>
> *(Genesis 35:30-3)*

We find that what's in Exodus 35:30-33 and Exodus 30:35 is the same as what's in Exodus 31:3-5, but in Exodus 30:34, Moses introduced Bezalel to the children of Israel with another aspect of his call that was not mentioned in Exodus 31. Exodus 35:34 states, *"And He has put in his heart the ability to teach, in him and Aholiab the son of Ahisamach, of the tribe of Dan.* This extra skill-set is "the ability to teach!"

We cannot deny that our God-given gifts are for more than just us to enjoy or hoard for ourselves. Our giftedness is also for us to pass on to others and teach them to do in excellence what we do. If we are to emulate Bezalel, the first man filled with the Spirit of Creativity, we must learn from him. You will also notice that the ability to teach was given to his destiny helper, Aholiab.

We cannot be hoarders of our gifts to monopolize the field we are in. I remember a story Francis shared with me early on in our marriage. A well-known man of God in the Body of Christ with thousands of followers once shared that he got many invitations to preach – more than enough to fill 365 days. He turned them away because he couldn't go to all of them. The Lord spoke to Francis and said, *I did not plan for him to turn these invitations away. He's supposed to have multiplied himself by now and sent those he trained to the places he could not go.* This man of God did not multiply and did not have a Aholiab in his camp.

We cannot be a hoarder of God's gifts given to us. We must multiply by teaching others our skills; I believe this is why God gave Bezalel the ability to teach. That means that it is in the heart of God to raise up Bezalels who are not just gifted in their craft, but also have the heart and compassion to teach and multiply. That should be our culture if we lead people as craftsmen. Those under us must also be trained to teach. I have expanded on our call to multiply in Chapter 10 of this book.

Our creativity for His glory

Now that we have learned about the importance of creativity in the life of a believer, I want to emphasize God's intent for the arts and the creative gifts He has given us. We learned earlier that the first man filled with His Spirit was an artist, or a craftsman. The first project God assigned him was to build God's sanctuary for Him to dwell among the Israelites.

This principle is integral to living in the creative realm. Our creativity must produce products that glorify God so that He can be seen throughout our work.

In Exodus 28:2, God instructed Moses to tell the skilled craftsmen, *"And you shall make holy garments for Aaron your brother, for glory and for beauty."* The word glory is from the Hebrew word, *kabowd*. This is very interesting, because the same word is used in 2 Chronicles 5:14 when the priests could not stand to minister and perform their service because of God's glory – His heavy and weighty presence that filled the temple.

You might ask,

> What is Carmela trying to convey here?

God wanted Aaron to wear a holy garment to release God's glory and beauty. Our creativity, therefore, must represent His glory and His beauty. It must be holy before the Lord.

It grieves my spirit whenever I read about stadiums being filled with people worshipping singers who sing secular songs full of profanity and dark messages, or when I see women wearing designer clothes meticulously conceived, sewn, and stitched to glorify the devil instead of God. In this regard, before we were introduced to Bezalel's call as a craftsman to build His sanctuary, God gave the Israelites the Ten Commandments (see Exodus 20). I want to emphasize verses 2 to 5 below:

I am the Lord your God, who brought you out of the land of Egypt, out of the house of bondage.

"You shall have no other gods before Me.

"You shall not make for yourself a carved image—any likeness of anything that is in heaven above, or that is in the earth beneath, or that is in the water under the earth;

"You shall not bow down to them nor serve them. For I, the Lord your God, am a jealous God, visiting the iniquity of the fathers upon the children to the third and fourth generations of those who hate Me."

As craftsmen, we must first remember that it was God who brought us out of bondage and gave us the ability to create. He commanded us to have no other gods and not make ourselves a carved image to idolize. Therefore, our creativity must produce products for the Kingdom, for Him, not for us. We cannot fall into satan's trap where we find ourselves bowing down and worshipping our creation instead of the Creator who gave us the ability to create it. We must be mindful that He is a jealous God (see verse 5) and we can't glorify our creativity above God by making our work an idol.

    I pray that you come to a place of total dependency on God by producing and creating products through which His beauty and glory can be seen.

Prayer of Release #2
– The Spirit of Creativity

Supernatural Decrees for Breakthrough

The Word says in Job 22:28, "decree a thing and it shall be established." Therefore,

- I decree and declare I have a renewed relationship with the Holy Spirit, who is the Spirit of Creativity, so I can discover every creative idea God has apportioned for me to manifest.

- I decree and declare that the creative genius God put in me emerges in this season of my life.

- I decree and declare that because I am filled with the Spirit of Creativity I operate in His wisdom, knowledge, understanding, and gifts in all manner of workmanship.

- I decree and declare that I operate in a higher level of discernment to discern those appointed by God to help me. I call forth my destiny helpers to assist me in every creative project God has called me to accomplish.

- I decree and declare that nothing I create will become my idol. I do not bow down and serve what I create, but I use it to expand His Kingdom and for His glory.

- I decree and declare that everything I produce through my God-given creative seeds is used for His glory.

- I decree and declare that I will not hoard my gifts, instead I will multiply by imparting them to others.

LIFE APPLICATION SECTION

Memory Verse

And Moses said to the children of Israel, "See, the Lord has called by name Bezalel the son of Uri, the son of Hur, of the tribe of Judah; and He has filled him with the Spirit of God, in wisdom and understanding, in knowledge and all manner of workmanship. *(Exodus 31:30-31)*

Reflections

1. Why did God appoint Bezalel to be in charge of building the Tabernacle?

2. Name the four types of destiny helpers? List the people in your life that are your destiny helpers.

CHAPTER 3

COMMUNION WITH THE SPIRIT OF CREATIVITY

> Creativity is the ability to discover and connect with our own God-given design, creative potential, and divine wisdom to create through communion with the Holy Spirit, who is the Spirit of Creativity.
>
> *(Carmela Myles)*

> As temples of the Holy Spirit, we should have communion with the Holy Spirit. The work of any believer is not only the work of a human individual but is actually the work of the Holy Spirit.
>
> *(Pope Shenouda III)*

> The grace of the Lord Jesus Christ, and the love of God, and the communion of the Holy Spirit be with you all. Amen.
>
> *(2 Corinthians 13:14)*

I must say this is the most crucial chapter in this book. This chapter holds the number one key to living in the creative realm. It is impossible to go through a life of creativity and fulfill our God-given assignment without having communion with the Holy Spirit. Apostle Paul's revelation on the Holy Spirit is seen in 2 Corinthians 13:14: *"The*

Communion with the Spirit of Creativity

grace of the Lord Jesus Christ, and the love of God, and the communion of the Holy Spirit be with you all. Amen."

Communion in this verse is from the Greek word *koinonia*, which means fellowship, sharing, and partnership. The Holy Spirit is not a thing; He is a person. You cannot possibly fellowship and have partnership with a thing unless it is a person.

When we become born again, the Holy Spirit comes to live inside of us and therefore He has access to our temple, which is now His abode. He doesn't need a key or a combination lock to get in. He is already living in us. Can you imagine living with another person who doesn't communicate at all? Husbands and wives can certainly understand that would be a problem.

I am writing this book because Francis heard the instruction from the Holy Spirit, who gave him the title of my book. As soon as I heard the title, *Living in the Creative Realm*, my spirit leaped, and I started running with it. If Francis did not have that relationship and communication with the Holy Spirit, this book would still be in the unseen realm.

Can you imagine if we had a constant and conscious realization of the existence of the Holy Spirit inside of us, how much revelation, guidance, and instruction we could experience? That is why fellowshipping and communing with the Holy Spirit is necessary. I wonder how the Holy Spirit feels when we don't engage Him in our day-to-day life, or when we don't communicate with Him? I don't doubt He is very excited to talk to us because of what He wants to share with us about our destiny, our assignment, and the creative ideas He wants to impart to us. I am sad to think how He feels as a Person when we ignore Him.

Many preachers have said He is probably the most ignored Person on earth. I concur. It is so easy to give praise and accolades to the voice and songs of Michael W. Smith; to the powerful teachings of Joyce Myer, and to the mighty miracles, signs, and wonders in Reinhard Bonke's ministry, but we never acknowledge the wisdom and the power behind them, which is the Holy Spirit flowing through them. He is behind every successful ministry, and His absence is why some ministries are no longer in existence.

Oh Lord, I pray for a new hunger in our lives to increase our fellowship with the Holy Spirit.

The Parakletos

We hear preachers call the Holy Spirit the *Parakletos*, but what do they mean by that term? According to John 14.26, *"But the Helper, the Holy Spirit, whom the Father will send in My name, He will teach you all things, and bring to your remembrance all things that I said to you."* The Helper here is from the Greek Word, *Parakletos*, defined as follows:

1. summoned, called to one's side, especially called to one's aid
   - one who pleads another's cause before a judge, a pleader, counsel for the defense, legal assistant, an advocate one who pleads another's cause with one, an intercessor;
   - of Christ in his exaltation at God's right hand, pleading with God the Father for the pardon of our sins;
   - in the broadest sense, a helper, succourer, aider, assistant; of the Holy Spirit destined to take the place of Christ with the apostles (after His ascension to the Father), to lead them to a deeper knowledge of the Gospel truth, and give them divine strength needed to enable them to undergo trials and persecutions on behalf of the divine kingdom.[2]

Parakletos is a legal term that means someone willing to stand beside us to contend legally against any accusations the enemy has against us in the Courts of Heaven. One of the primary wiles of the enemy is to rob us of our legal rights by derailing us from our Book of Destiny by making us ignorant of the existence of the Courts of Heaven.

The next chapter of this book is on the Book of Destiny for you to gain a better understanding of our Book of Destiny. There might be some legal accusations that are hindering you from being activated in your creativity that are written in your Book of Destiny.

The good news is that we have the *Parakletos*, who also pleads our cause by acting as our intercessor. He intercedes for us to ensure that a divine acquittal permanently removes the enemy's legal rights against us from the Courts of Heaven. Again, this is one of the reasons why we must have communion with the Holy Spirit.

The Courts of Heaven are not my topic here, but there are many books on this subject by Robert Henderson and my husband, Dr. Francis Myles, to have further understanding of them.

Sealed with the Holy Spirit

According to Ephesians 1:13-14, "*In Him you also trusted, after you heard the word of truth, the gospel of your salvation; in whom also, having believed, you were sealed with the Holy Spirit of promise, who is the guarantee of our inheritance until the redemption of the purchased possession, to the praise of His glory.*"

Not only is He a person, but we are also sealed by Him. He is the guarantor of our inheritance – everything that was promised to us. The word guarantee is from the Greek word *arrhabon*, which means an earnest, or a deposit, a part of the payment given in advance as a security that the whole will be paid afterward.

Ponder this: the Holy Spirit was sent as an advance payment to secure our inheritance. God the Father didn't send our parents, relatives, friends, pastors or our government officials. Instead, He sent us the Holy Spirit of promise. This is very deep! The Scripture gives us full assurance of our inheritance, so there is no reason for us to doubt, or be afraid of what is ahead. Instead we should be confident because we have the Holy Spirit who backs us up. He was sent to stand alongside us to secure our inheritance.

In our world, unless someone gives us a gift, no one will hand us a key to a house or a car without a deposit. Any lending company or bank has to check our credit to ensure that we are qualified before we are even allowed to drive a car off a car lot, or given a key to occupy, even if it's only a $100,000 house. We have to go through a grueling process of submitting multiple documents to prove that we can pay the mortgage. The bank and mortgage companies have to make sure that they will not get duped by handing over an asset that we might not be able to pay back later.

Therefore, if a person here on earth has the key to our inheritance and serves as a guarantor to secure it, I bet we would do anything to make sure we have a solid relationship, fellowship, and partnership with that person. Who wouldn't?

Fellowship with the Holy Spirit, who is the Spirit of Creativity

Similarly, if you wanted to learn and become an expert in your field of creativity, wouldn't you want to be the student of a master who could mentor you to become one of the best? To live in the creative realm, it is a necessity to fellowship with the Holy Spirit. Jesus, the "pattern Son" – the one who showed us how to relate to the Father and to the Holy Spirit – operated in this realm while He was on earth.

> Therefore, if there is any consolation in Christ, if any comfort of love, if any fellowship of the Spirit, if any affection and mercy, fulfill my joy by being like-minded, having the same love, being of one accord, of one mind. Let nothing be done through selfish ambition or conceit, but in lowliness of mind let each esteem others better than himself. Let each of you look out not only for his own interests, but also for the interests of others. Let this mind be in you which was also in Christ Jesus, who, being in the form of God, did not consider it robbery to be equal with God, but made Himself of no reputation, taking the form of a bondservant, and coming in the likeness of

men. And being found in appearance as a man, He humbled Himself and became obedient to the point of death, even the death of the cross.

(Philippians 2:1-8)

In these verses, we find that Jesus' fellowship and communion with the Holy Spirit resulted in the godly attributes listed below. I believe we must emulate these attributes to live in the creative realm:

- He became like-minded
- He overcame selfish-ambition
- He attained lowliness of mind
- He looked after others
- He made Himself of no reputation
- He became humble
- He became obedient

Two Scriptures about Jesus have always affected me: John 5:19 and John 4:34.

In John 4:34 it states: *"Jesus said to them, 'My food is to do the will of Him who sent Me, and to finish His work.'"* He also said, according to John 5:19, *"Most assuredly, I say to you, the Son can do nothing of Himself, but what He sees the Father do; for whatever He does, the Son also does in like manner."*

I pondered these two Scriptures and came up with the stages we must go through to fulfill our God-given assignment and start living in the creative realm.

The Stages in finishing our assignment by imitating the "pattern Son" to live in the creative realm:

1. **Jesus first acknowledged His sonship and His relationship with God as His Father** – Jesus played many roles while He was

here on earth: He was a deliverer, our Savior, a Prophet, Apostle, and Healer. But in this passage of the Scripture, He emphasized His role as a "pattern Son."

For many of us to finish our assignment, we need to get the revelation that we are a "son." We cannot possibly approach God as Father if we do not get the revelation that we are His "son" (*son* refers to women also – there is no gender in the spirit). We cannot just go to our principal in high school and expect him to pay our school fees. It is the responsibility of our parents. We will approach everyone else instead of Him as our Father if we don't have a revelation that we are His sons.

Most earthly parents want their children to be the best. I have seen them do anything to ensure their children are taken care of and have the necessary skills to live successfully here on earth.

If our earthly parents have that desire, how much more does our heavenly Father? He has put great resources in us to create products to expand His Kingdom. I believe that the understanding of being His son allows us to discover these products and the creativity He deposited in us before we were even born.

2. **Jesus understood that He was sent** – He did not leave heaven because He felt like going; the Father sent Him. I believe that one of the reasons we experience mishaps and unfulfilled assignments is because we go where our Father never sent us.

Why do we do it?

3. **Jesus ate eternal food** – *"My food is to do the will of Him who sent Me, and to finish His work"* (John 4:34). According to this Scripture, Jesus "ate" two eternal foods, namely:

a. *The will of the Father who sent Him* – Jesus "ate" the will of His Father! He "ate" the will of the Father even when it was hard for Him. To better understand this statement, let's go to Luke 22:42, where we see Jesus saying, *"Father, if it is Your will, take this cup away from Me; nevertheless, not My will, but Yours, be done."*

It is apparent from this passage that Jesus didn't want to take the cup of going to the Cross. However, going to the Cross was the will of His Father, and it aligned with His Book of Destiny, therefore, it had to be done. It was a must – a divine necessity – for Him to partake of this "food."

This is the type of "food" we must learn to eat every day to guarantee the fulfillment of our assignments. It is a food that will also lead to our own cross. Pride is the only thing that can prevent us from eating the will of God our Father. In the presence of pride, we partake of our own food made up of our own will. That is precisely the opposite of what God wants us to do. I can guarantee that the food of our own will lead to indigestion. We will feel like vomiting because the food of our will put knots in our stomachs from unnecessary stress and anxiety over what we ate. It didn't align with His will. The question is,

What cup is God asking you to partake of at this time?

Is it adopting a child; or giving up your music or acting career? Is it selling your business or giving away your house? Whatever it is, it's certainly a choice that will lead us to our cross, so that like Jesus, we will have to ask the Father to take it away from us.

We must not waste the food our Father in heaven is asking us to eat. We must come to that place where our answer should be like that of Jesus: *"Nevertheless not my will, but Yours, be done!"*

May we all come to this place!

    b. *To finish the Father's work* – Jesus also "ate" the food of finishing the work of His Father. This food assured Him the completion of His assignment. He died on the Cross so you and I can come back to the Father.

4. **Jesus can do nothing of Himself** – Jesus understood that apart from God, we cannot do anything out of our own strength. Therefore, it's always good to acknowledge that we have what we have because it was given to us from above. Otherwise, pride can tap us on the back and whisper that our gain was all because of what we did!

5. **Jesus only did what He saw the Father doing** – Our actions should always mirror what our Father is doing. That is probably one of the most demanding challenges we as believers face every day regarding our walk with God.

6. **Jesus does things exactly in the same manner in which He saw the Father doing them** – Jesus not only did what He saw the Father was doing, but He did it <u>exactly</u> in the way and manner the Father was doing it!

We must understand these stages of finishing our assignment to live in the creative realm. I encourage you to increase your interaction with the Holy Spirit intentionally so that you can accomplish all He has for you here on earth.

Communion with the Spirit of Creativity

Lord, first of all, thank You for giving me the gift of Your Holy Spirit. Thank You for His gift of guidance and service to me as my intercessor and advocate, always to stand alongside me to ensure I don't miss Your mark! I decree and declare that I have Your divine grace to fellowship with the Holy Spirit. Give me an increased sensitivity to the Holy Spirit that I don't ignore Him in all I do. I repent for ignoring Your Holy Spirit in me and for not including Him in my decisions, for going ahead of Him or procrastinating in following His leading, and for not being consistent in my interaction with Him. Lord, make me like Jesus, that I will only eat the food He ate, which is Your will for my life, that I will stay in alignment and never divert from Your will for me. Lord, I desire to come to that place and acknowledge that I cannot do anything unless You give it to me. I pray and declare this in the mighty Name of Jesus!

Prayer of Release #3
– Communion with the Holy Spirit

Supernatural Decrees for Breakthrough

The Word says in Job 22:28, "decree a thing and it shall be established," therefore,

- I decree and declare that my relationship with the Holy Spirit, who is the Spirit of Creativity, causes exponential blessings to be released in my life because of my fellowship, partnership, and communion with Him.

- I decree and declare that I only do what I see my Father doing so that I finish what He asks of me.

- I decree and declare that I am sealed with the Holy Spirit. He is the Guarantor of my inheritance; therefore, my inheritance is secured, and the enemy cannot steal it from me or the generation after me.

- I decree and declare that the Holy Spirit is my *Parakletos*. He always stands alongside me to ensure that I am acquitted of all accusations the enemy has against me. My assignments will not be hindered, but shall be accomplished.

- I decree and declare I have the supernatural grace to stay humble because I can accomplish nothing unless the Holy Spirit operates through me. My gifts all came from Him and all praise and glory belong to Him.

- I decree and declare that I will finish my Father's work.

LIFE APPLICATION SECTION

Memory Verse

But the Helper, the Holy Spirit, whom the Father will send in My name, He will teach you all things, and bring to your remembrance all things that I said to you. *(John 14:26)*

Reflections

1. What do you mean by *Parakletos*?

   _____
   _____
   _____
   _____
   _____

2. What does it mean to be sealed by the Holy Spirit?

   _____
   _____
   _____
   _____
   _____

CHAPTER 4

THE BOOK OF DESTINY – OUR DIVINE DESIGN

Creativity is the ability to discover and connect with our own God-given design, creative potential and divine wisdom to create through the communion with the Holy Spirit, who is the Spirit of Creativity.

(Carmela Myles)

Your eyes saw my substance, being yet unformed. And in Your Book, they all were written, the days fashioned for me, when as yet there were none of them.

(Psalm 139:16)

Design is intelligence made visible.

(Alina Wheeler, Author)

Before I expand on the Book of Destiny, let me first define what *design* means.

According to *Encyclopedia.com*, design is a plan, or drawing produced to show the look and function, or workings of a building, garment, or other object before it is built or made. According to *Merriam-Webster Dictionary*, design is:

- to conceive and plan out in the mind
- to create, fashion, execute, or construct according to plan
- to have as a purpose
- to devise for a specific function or end

Based on the definitions in *Encylopedia.com* and in *Merriam-Webster Dictionary*, I came up with this statement:

> You were conceived in the mind of our Creator and He has strategically planned and designed you for a specific function to fulfill His purpose before you were even built and made!

God's strategic plan for us

I always tell people that the King of all kings, Lord of all Lords, our heavenly Father strategically planned and intricately conceived our design for His purpose, *"For I know the plans and thoughts that I have for you,' says the LORD, 'plans for peace and well-being and not for disaster, to give you a future and a hope"* (Jeremiah 29:11, AMP). All of His plans for us were written in His Book of Destiny. Those plans are for us to prosper and live in peace without disaster befalling our lives.

According to Psalm 139:14, God fearfully and wonderfully made us. The word fearfully is from the Hebrew word *Yare* which means to fear and be afraid of, but it also means reverence and honor.

How can the God of all creation fear and be afraid? Due to the reverence and honor He has for man, I can only say that our God, who intricately thought of and created each one of us, was "afraid" in the following sense as He was creating us: He was careful and deeply thoughtful in every aspect of our creation. We might say an artist is "afraid" of making a mistake, or especially careful not to mess up the face of a person he is painting on canvas, or a sculptor makes sure he is chiseling stone the right way so its shape will not be distorted.

I believe it's safe to say that based on the design our Creator was using to make us, we would come out perfect, the way He planned us in His mind. By the time we manifested into existence, we were a masterpiece – a wonder. In the same passage the Psalmist said, *"I am wonderfully made"* (Psalm 139:14).

What an amazing declaration of how David believed himself to be! Similarly, you and I are also not just fearfully made, we are also wonderfully made. Wonderfully is from the Hebrew word *Parah*, which means "separated or distinct." We are a wonder on this earth because there is no one like us. We are meant to be set apart and distinct so that when the world sees u̲s and comes into our presence, it should immediately notice that we are not the same – we are different.

Have you ever been to the Niagara Falls or Victoria Falls? Or any of the Seven Wonders of the world? When you see these places, your eyes light up, you gape with your mouth open, and you gasp at the beauty of how it was created. This type of reaction should be what we should expect when others (believers or not) come into our presence because we are a wonder, and the product we create should follow in the same order!

Our Book of Destiny

Our divine legal rights

It is very important for all believers to understand that each one of us has a Book of Destiny. It establishes our legal rights before God. Why is this important?

Understanding our legal rights gives us the ability to fight for what is legally ours. One of the enemy's plots or wiles is to prevent us from fulfilling our purpose by making sure we don't discover what is in our Book. Then instead of trying to discover what is already in our Book, we end up sweating and toiling to create our destiny based on what we think it should be. As a result, we find ourselves doing things and being involved with unnecessary activities that most likely are not in our Book. We end up in situations that don't align with God's plan for our lives.

Some of us marry the wrong person. A friend of mine was pursued by a man who wasn't really walking with the Lord, but once he found out her passion for God, he started carrying a Bible. They got married, and all hell broke out during the first day of their honeymoon. She was miserable with him.

Some become involved in wrong business ventures, promoting and selling the wrong products.

I am sure many of you can relate. I graduated in the wrong course as an accountant and became a Certified Public Accountant (CPA) in the State of New York. I was hired by one of the Big Four Accounting firms to work in Manhattan. I made a very good salary, but I found out that I couldn't stand it. The whole time I was working there, I was miserable and frustrated. Now I am big on encouraging people to discover what is in their Book of Destiny. It will save them from going around the mountain again and again without a destination in sight.

Since I became a believer, I have been fascinated with Psalm 139:16 – one of the well-known songs of King David, specifically when he talked about how our days were fashioned and ordained for us, and how they were written in God's Book before any of them came to be.

Thus even before we were born, God had already written everything about us in His Book. As a new believer I meditated on this Scripture and always thought about God having a Book – one like a scroll on which there were words, sentences, paragraphs and chapters about me and my life, written before I was even born.

Ten the Lord showed me Jeremiah 1:5, *"Before I formed you in the womb, I knew you; Before you were born, I sanctified you; I ordained you a prophet to the nations."*

As soon as I came upon this Scripture, I connected it perfectly to Psalm 139:16, because it amplified my understanding of this passage. Jeremiah shared how God knew him before he was formed in his mother's womb. Before he was formed, means before he was conceived and existed – before he transcended from the spirit realm into the natural realm, and before God took him out of the spirit realm and put him into his human body. I asked God: "Are you telling me that before I was born, you knew me? How is that possible?"

These questions led me to dig deeper. I found out that *yada* is the Hebrew word for *knew*. *Yada* means to know, to perceive, to know by experience, and to know intimately. Knowing God intimately is like a husband and wife knowing each other intimately. Three Scriptures I found prove the meaning of the word *yada* as follows:

- And Adam knew Eve his wife; and she conceived, and bare Cain, and said, I have gotten a man from the LORD. *(Genesis 4:1)*

- And Cain knew his wife; and she conceived, and bare Enoch: and he builded a city, and called the name of the city, after the name of his son, Enoch. *(Genesis 4:17)*

- And Adam knew his wife again; and she bare a son, and called his name Seth: For God, said she, hath appointed me another seed instead of Abel, whom Cain slew. *(Genesis 4:25)*

The above Scriptures are very clear. The word *yada* describes knowing someone in an intimate and sexual way. Adam *yada* Eve his wife, and she conceived and gave birth to Cain; Cain *yada* his wife, and she conceived and gave birth to Enoch, and lastly, Adam *yada* his wife again, and gave birth to another son, and they called him Seth.

I don't know about you, but there is no way you can intimately *yada* your husband or your wife without touching them, seeing them, hearing them and smelling them. Similarly, we cannot *yada* God and not touch Him, see Him, smell Him and hear Him. This is very clear. Before we were conceived in our mother's womb, we saw God, touched Him, smelled Him and heard Him.

Our intimacy with God is the reason why Jeremiah 1:5 is very crucial in understanding the existence of our Book of Destiny.

God told Jeremiah that before he was born that He sanctified him and appointed him to be a prophet to the nations. Now that we understand what *yada* means, we can be certain that Jeremiah had a private conversation with God. He heard that he was sanctified before he was born.

I challenge you to apply this principle to your life. If God told Jeremiah that he was sanctified before he was born, you have to believe that you also have been sanctified, consecrated and set apart for Him before you were born. Most important, we also learned God ordained him in heaven before he was born according to what He had called him to be on earth. Jeremiah was ordained a prophet to the nations. The questions are:

What was your conversation with God before you were born?

What did He ordain you to be?

We all have one thing in common. We all came on earth through a fallen womb. As a result, we have forgotten our private conversations with God and what He ordained us to be. Praise God for the redeeming love of our Lord Jesus Christ that through His obedience and shed blood we can be reconnected to our heavenly Father. Praise Him also for the Holy Spirit who can put back into our remembrance the conversations we had with God, our Father.

The five questions we must answer

The Holy Spirit can open our spiritual eyes so we can see and read what is written in our Book of Destiny. In the Book of Destiny, we find answers to the five questions we need answered to live our lives effectively here on earth. These questions are integral to fulfilling our purpose and understanding our destiny. They help us know which race to run and which mountain to climb. It would be a complete waste of time and energy to win a gold medal for being the first one to cross the finish line, or reach the top of the mountain, only to find out that we were in the wrong race or had climbed the wrong mountain. That gold medal means nothing in heaven! This is what happens to those who do not know what's in their Book of Destiny. They end up doing things they are not supposed to do, and hence find themselves competing in the wrong race and climbing the wrong mountain. It reminds me of a story of a Pastor of a successful church.

When the pastor had an encounter with the Lord, He told him that even though he has a successful church, He had never asked him to pastor one! People of earth might rejoice at what appear to be our great achievements, and man's accolades might be music to our ears, but they would be clanging cymbals to the cloud of witnesses and heaven's army. We don't need to create our destiny. Instead, we need to discover what is already written in our Book so we can answer these questions and avoid this outcome. Here are the five questions.

1. **Where did you come from (your Source)?** This is a question of our origin and Source. If we don't know our Source, we cannot discover our identity, purpose, potential and ultimate destination. According to Jeremiah 1:5, God was the One who formed us in our mother's womb, and in Genesis 1:26-28, we see that God was the one who created us:

   > Then God said, "Let Us make man in Our image, according to Our likeness; let them have dominion over the fish of the sea, over the birds of the air, and over the cattle, over all the earth and over every creeping thing that creeps on the earth." So God created man in His own image; in the image of God He created him; male and female He created them. Then God blessed them, and God said to them, "Be fruitful and

multiply; fill the earth and subdue it; have dominion over the fish of the sea, over the birds of the air, and over every living thing that moves on the earth.

2. **Who are you (your Identity)?** This question gives us understanding of our uniqueness and what makes us different from the person sitting next to us. Our identity must not be based on our talents, education, gifts or positions. It must be based on who we are in God. The sooner we discover that our identity is not based on these things, but on the One who created us, the sooner we can determine our purpose of why God sent us from His presence to earth and put us in a physical body. This prevents us from taking the path of comparing ourselves to others and from striving to prove our worth. Instead, we become at peace with who we are, knowing we can do whatever task He gives us.

3. **Why are you here (your Purpose)?** This question determines our purpose. According to *Lexico.com*, purpose "is the reason for which something is done or created, or for which something exists." Therefore, our existence is not happenstance. Isaiah 46:10-11 states:

> Declaring the end and the result from the beginning, And from ancient times the things which have not [yet] been done, Saying, 'My purpose will be established, And I will do all that pleases Me and fulfills My purpose,' Calling a bird of prey from the east, from a far country, the man (Cyrus) of My purpose. Truly I have spoken; truly I will bring it to pass. I have planned it, be assured I will do.

Cyrus was called from a far country. God even referred to him as a "bird of prey from the east" to specify his purpose on earth.

We are all created to fulfill a purpose – His, not ours! The question is:

What is the purpose for which we are created?

This is a question many believers haven't answered yet, or have struggled to answer. The answer is in our heavenly Book!

4. **What can we do (your Potential)?** Potential is expressed through ability. God didn't create us without potential and ability to fulfill our purpose. Its discovery releases the gifts and talents hidden in all of us – ones we don't even know we have.

5. **Where are you going (your Destiny)?** If we don't know where we are going, we won't even know we have arrived. I believe we can be confident we are on the right path to our destination when everything converges – our purpose and potential merge with our divine design to arrive at the conclusion of our Book.

All of His creation is waiting and groaning for our appearing as sons of God. It is eagerly and earnestly looking forward to seeing the real you and me. Why?

When Adam and Eve fell out of God's Kingdom, creation also fell with them. Our appearing will release creation out of its bondage so it can also fulfill God's original intent for its existence.

Consider this: a lion wasn't created to eat another animal; a mouse wasn't intended to be food for cats. What about those nasty mosquitoes that cause some of us to scratch swollen bites? Could their original purpose have been to bite us? That's hard to imagine.

Neither was an ant created to bite us. It wasn't purposed to be a nuisance. We might not be able to stand having ants around, but we are oblivious to their many functions. According to *thoughtco.com*, ants aerate soil and improve its drainage: "As ants build nests and construct tunnels in the ground, they improve the soil significantly. They redistribute nutrients as they move soil particles from place to place, and the voids created by their tunnels improve air and water circulation in the soil."

My prayer is for you to be able to answer these five questions, have a deeper revelation of your Source, find your identity, discover your purpose, maximize your potential, and arrive at your destination.

Prayer of Release #4
– The Book of Destiny: Our Divine Design

Supernatural Decrees for Breakthrough

The Word says in Job 22:28, "decree a thing and it shall be established," therefore,

- I decree and declare that I was conceived in the mind of my Creator and He strategically planned and designed me for a specific function to fulfill His purpose. Therefore, everything I do reflects His design.

- I decree and declare Jeremiah 29:11 over my life, *"For I know the plans and thoughts that I have for you,' says the LORD, 'plans for peace and well-being and not for disaster, to give you a future and a hope."* Therefore, I have peace that my life has a future and a hope.

- I acknowledge that I have a Book of Destiny, and my Book was written before I was even born. Therefore, I purpose in my heart to fulfill every page of my Book.

- I decree and declare that my spiritual eyes are open to read what is in my Book; my spiritual ears are open to hear what God has separated and appointed for me to do, and I decree that I will remember every conversation with God before He sent me here on earth.

- I decree and declare that there is no longer any confusion in my life because I know where I came from; I know who I am; I know my purpose; I know my abilities and capacities, and I know the direction where I am going.

- I decree and declare that all of creation is eagerly and earnestly looking forward to seeing the real me. Creation rejoices as it sees the real version of me emerge.

LIFE APPLICATION SECTION

Memory Verse

But the Helper, the Holy Spirit, whom the Father will send in My name, He will teach you all things, and bring to your remembrance all things that I said to you. *(John 14:26)*

Reflections

1. What is your divine design?

2. What are the five questions that we must answer to discover what is in our Book of Destiny?

CHAPTER 5

OUR GOD-GIVEN DIVINE POTENTIAL

> Creativity is the ability to discover and connect with our own God-given design, <u>creative potential</u>, and divine wisdom through the communion with the Holy Spirit, who is the Spirit of Creativity.
>
> *(Carmela Myles)*

> Believe in your infinite potential. Your only limitations are those you set upon yourself.
>
> *(Roy T. Bennett)*

Heaven rejoices when the mind of God is manifested on earth, when His creation discovers its destiny and produces what is in its Book of Destiny, and when His purpose and plan for creation are fulfilled.

So, what was in the mind of God when He created man?

Genesis 1:26 states, *"Then God said, "Let Us make man in Our image, according to Our likeness; let them have dominion over the fish of the sea, over the birds of the air, and over the cattle, over all the earth and over every creeping thing that creeps on the earth."*

Dominion, in this passage, means to reign, rule, dominate and prevail against.

The Kingdom mandate of man was beautifully painted on the canvas of this passage. Man was given a Kingdom mandate to have dominion – to rule and reign over the earth and every living creature on it. Being created in the image and likeness of God assures us that we were not created to fail, because failure does not exist in God. It is not in His vocabulary, or His nature, and is far from His original intent for man. He will never give us a mandate without a plan and provision to fulfill it. Of all His creations, man was the only one created in the image and likeness of God. It is His provision – the evidence of His Divine plan. It is an assurance that the mandate of the Kingdom will be fulfilled and completed through man.

God has deposited so much inside of us, yet many of us cannot fathom the depth of our creative and divine potential. Even if we are given a glimpse of the treasures He deposited in us, our human mind cannot comprehend, or even imagine the magnitude of it all.

Though it is certainly there, we can't manifest something we don't believe. Doubt will always trespass in our minds to convince us that we don't have the ability and capacity to fulfill His mandate. These deposits God has made in us mean nothing if they remain dormant and unused. The only way we can escape the prison cell of dormancy, stagnation, and doubt is if we have a revelation of who we are, where we came from, and to whom we belong.

So, who are we?
Where did we come from?
To whom do we belong?

Let's go back to Genesis 1:26. This Scripture is our ticket to understanding what was in the mind of God when He took us out of eternity and put us in our earthly body. This passage explains the good news that we were created in the image and likeness of an omnipotent God.

Our God-Given Divine Potential

What does it mean?

The word omnipotent comes from two Latin words, *omnis*, meaning all, and *potentia* or *potens*, meaning power. Hence, the God of the Bible is the God of all power. Man was created by an *Omnis potens* and *Omnis potentia* God!

It's very interesting that the origin of the word potential also came from the same root word: *potentia*. Therefore, it is safe to say that God is an Omni-Potential God! If man was created in the image and likeness of an Omni-Potential God, then man also has all the power and potential to fulfill his Kingdom mandate.

We are remiss if we think we are powerless and cannot be the solution God created us to be. It is the greatest deception of the enemy to make us believe otherwise. God created every man with a specific purpose and assignment in mind. He is a Master Strategist with a well-thought-out plan – a plan that includes the provision (potential) necessary to complete the assignment.

What is potential?

According to *Merriam-Webster Dictionary*, potential is "existing in possibility; capable of development into actuality and potential benefits." If you say that someone, or something has potential, you mean that they have the necessary abilities, or qualities to become successful or useful in the future. Therefore, potential refers to hidden talents, qualities, and abilities. Potential is God's original intent that existed in His mind for someone's life before He formed him in his mother's womb.

- It is untapped capacity and dormant ability.
- It is what a person is capable of becoming before he has even discovered it.
- It's the thing someone was born to do before he has even achieved it.

- It is what is seen in heaven, but yet unseen on earth.
- It is man's future trapped within him.

Thus potential is the hidden or dormant talents, gifts, abilities, and qualities that must be discovered to fulfill and complete someone's mandate and purpose.

If something is hidden, it needs to be discovered. If something is dormant, it needs to be awakened and released from suspension.

Most people are still in a deep sleep, suspended and parked on their shelves of despair, pain, and unworthiness. They are emotionally distraught from the circumstances of life and past failures. Their past is like a swamp that attracts mosquitoes that continuously bite them. These bites are nuisances blinding them from seeing who they truly are.

It is impossible to find our purpose if we are still living in our swamp where trauma, pain, and hopelessness are always biting us.

Unleashing your potential

To discover and maximize our potential, we need to understand God's creative process. In Chapter 2, I dealt with the process of creation when the substance already exists. Here I am dealing with the process of creating called *Bara* – creating from nothing.

1. The process starts with a problem God wants to solve.
2. He strategically devises a solution to the problem by creating a creature to be an answer to it.
3. The problem becomes the reason and purpose for this being's creation.
4. God puts the solution inside that creature, and that purpose is what determines its ability.
5. He then decides what material substance or source to use to create the solution.
6. He speaks to that source or material substance.

7. When the final creation is brought into existence, it already possesses the substance needed to solve the problem it was created to solve.

Let us go back to the account of creation in Genesis 1 to see how that process unfolded.

When God decided to create vegetation, He spoke to the earth and said, *"Let there be vegetation, every plant, every fruit-bearing tree, let it be."* And, what happened? The vegetation came out of where? The dirt – the earth.

When He wanted to have marine life and every sea creature, He spoke to the water and said, *"Let the water bring forth the fish, and the marine life and the whales and everything that moves in the ocean."* So, marine life came forth.

When He decided He wanted animals, what did He do? He spoke to the earth and said, *"Let there be all the cattle and every moving creature, the beast of the earth, the elephants, lions, monkeys came out of the earth."*

The potential of a creature comes from the substance from which it was created. That is its source. If it is detached from its source, not only does it weaken its potential, it is threatened with extinction. The fish's ability is maximized when it swims because water is the source of its potential. If the fish decides to come out of the water, it will die because swimming in water is the nature of the fish.

Vegetation's ability to produce fruit is maximized when it is planted in the earth. If a plant is uprooted from the earth, it will wither and eventually die. Albert Einstein once said, "Everyone is a genius. But if you judge a fish by its ability to climb a tree, it will live its whole life believing that it is stupid." The fish's ability is in the water, not in climbing a tree.

> So, what about man?
> How did He create man?

When He decided to create man, He did not speak to the earth; He did not speak to the water or the firmament. He spoke to Himself. And He said, "Let Us make man in Our image and in Our likeness," so the source of our potential is in God Himself because He spoke to Himself and created us in His image and likeness. Our potential comes out of Him!

A spirit is illegal on earth unless it has a body. He therefore also spoke to the earth so man could have a body. He had to create something physical so man could stay here on earth. He made man a body out of the dirt to house its spirit.

Our body is made out of dirt, but our spirit is made out of His Spirit.

Our potential to function through our body is limited because it is made from the earth, but our potential is unlimited by the Spirit. As Paul explained to the Corinthians, *"Therefore we do not lose heart. Even though our outward man is perishing, yet the inward man is being renewed day by day."* (2 Corinthians 4:16)

It is very difficult for someone to believe in his unlimited potential without a revelation of his creation. He will always focus on his perceived ability (or inability) and not His source. His thoughts will always focus on his disability – that he has been molested, divorced, and emotionally damaged. It will be the same for a 90-year-old who thinks his time has come because his body can no longer function as it once did. Similarly, a 20-year-old who has been trampled and stepped on, might lose hope to believe he can make it to the following year despite his youth.

The condition of our physical body should never be a deterrent from unleashing our potential to discover the untapped creativity that God has put in us. If we are still alive, kicking, and breathing, it means there is still more for us to do. Hence, there is still creative potential in each of us that the world needs for solving its problems. The purpose of God cannot be stopped. According to Job 42.2, *"I know that You can do everything and that no purpose of Yours can be withheld from You."* Consider this:

- Moses was 80 when he led Israel out of Egypt;
- Caleb was 83 when he fought to take possession of his inheritance;
- Miguel de Cervantes was in his late 50s when he wrote 'Don Quixote';
- Grandma Moses was 78 when she put paint on canvas for the first time;
- Ray Kroc opened the first McDonald's restaurant at age 53;
- Laura Ingalls Wilder was 65 when the first book in her *Little House on the Prairie* series was published;
- Leo Goodwin founded GEICO, an insurance company, at the age of 50, and,
- Colonel Sanders franchised Kentucky Fried Chicken for the first time at 62.

If we don't know our Source (God), or if we detach from our Source, we will not be able to fulfill our potential because our potential is connected to our Source. Jesus said it this way in John 15:5: *"I am the vine, you are the branches. He who abides in Me, and I in him, bears much fruit; for without Me you can do nothing."*

If people give up before their appointed time instead of asking God, their Source, what was in His mind when He created them, then wasted potential will be buried in many graves. So, the question is,

What are the hidden potentials inside you that need to be unleashed so you can create what God has given you to produce?

Prayer of Release #5
– Our Creative Potential

Supernatural Decrees for Breakthrough

The Word says in Job 22:28, "decree a thing and it shall be established," therefore,

- I decree and declare that God created me with a specific purpose and assignment. He is my Master Strategist with a well-thought-out plan that includes all provision, including my potential, necessary to complete my assignment.

- I decree and declare that I was created by an *Omnis potens* and *Omnis potentia* God. Therefore, I have much untapped capability and dormant ability.

- I decree and declare that I will discover every hidden potential God has put in me. I will die empty, for every potential He put in me will manifest.

- I decree and declare that God is my Source in all things, therefore He is the Source of my potential.

- I decree and declare that the condition of my physical body will never be a deterrent to unleashing my potential to discover the untapped creativity that God put in me. As long as I am alive, there is more for me to do.

- I acknowledge that the talents, gifts, and potential God deposited in me mean nothing if they remain dormant and unused. The only way I can escape the prison cell of dormancy, stagnation and doubt is if I have a revelation of who I am, where I came from, and to whom I belong. I decree and declare that God created me and deposited my potential in me. I belong to Him.

- I decree and declare that it is never too late. I will perform everything God called me to do regardless of my age.

LIFE APPLICATION SECTION

Memory Verse

I am the vine, you are the branches. He who abides in Me, and I in him, bears much fruit; for without Me you can do nothing. *(John 15:5)*

Reflections

1. What is the potential?

2. What is the process of creating something out of nothing?

CHAPTER 6

OUR INNATE WISDOM

> Creativity is the ability to discover and connect with our God-given design, creative potential, and the <u>divine wisdom</u> to create through communion with the Holy Spirit, who is the Spirit of Creativity.
>
> *(Carmela Myles)*

> O Lord, how many and varied are Your works
> In wisdom You have made them all;
> The earth is full of Your riches and Your creatures.
>
> *(Psalm 104:24, AMP)*

From this chapter I want us to understand that God will not give us any idea without His corresponding divine wisdom to create it. Therefore, when we start to live in the creative realm, we will also discover the God-given wisdom that He has deposited in us to manifest our assignments. In studying the Bible we will find that God's wisdom is linked to creation, which means that God will not create anything without wisdom.

In Psalm 104:24, the Psalmist states clearly that God created everything in wisdom: *"O Lord, how many and varied are Your works! In wisdom You have made them all; The earth is full of Your riches and Your creatures."* His works are many and varied. They were all created in wisdom, and all means *all!*

Everything that God has created was with wisdom. Jeremiah, by revelation, also understood that the earth was established by His wisdom: *"God made the earth by His power; He established the world by His wisdom. And by His understanding and skill He has stretched out the heavens"* (Jeremiah 10:12).

Jeremiah also confirmed what the Psalmist said: the world was established by His wisdom.

If the Master Creator needed wisdom to create and establish the earth, then we also need wisdom to create and establish whatever God has already purposed for us.

It is a fact that we cannot establish anything without His wisdom. That is why I am very excited to bring forth this understanding, because we should be able to activate His wisdom when we live in the creative realm. We should not fret or be discouraged if we feel that we lack wisdom to create. In James 1:5, God urges us to ask for wisdom, *"If any of you lacks wisdom, let him ask of God, who gives to all liberally and without reproach, and it will be given to him."*

There it is! If we don't have wisdom, then we should ask for it! Not only will He give it to us liberally, or generously, but God will also give it to us without judgment, criticism, or guilt. Why? He knows without a shadow of the doubt that we cannot create without divine wisdom, so He has to give it without any reproach.

If we find a store owner who will never say No every time we go to his store and ask him for free candy, we will always be there to ask for more. This should be our disposition concerning acquiring wisdom from God. We should always go to God to ask for His wisdom.

If you are a tailor, ask for wisdom to create a new style of clothing that could make you become a brand-name designer. If you are an author, ask for wisdom to write about a topic that can change your nation's culture to align with God's Kingdom. If you are a stay-home mom who loves to bake, then ask Him for wisdom to create one of the best pies you can bake while your baby is sleeping.

What wisdom do you need?

Start asking now, because He will not deny any of us who ask for it. As James said, He gives to *all*. All means *all!*

Spiritual wisdom

> However, we speak wisdom among those who are mature, yet not the wisdom of this age, nor of the rulers of this age, who are coming to nothing. But we speak the wisdom of God in a mystery, the hidden wisdom which God ordained before the ages for our glory, which none of the rulers of this age knew; for had they known, they would not have crucified the Lord of glory.
>
> *(1 Corinthians 2:6-7)*

In the passage of the Scripture above, we find Paul talking about three different types of wisdom:

1. *Wisdom of this age* – According to Paul, this wisdom comes to nothing. Paul also talks about a span of time and the wisdom of their day. Today our generation is presented with issues like Black Lives Matter, legalized abortions, cancel culture, and transgenderism, among other cultural controversies that do not align with the wisdom of the Kingdom.

2. *Wisdom of the rulers of this age* – According to Paul, this wisdom also comes to nothing! It is wisdom without discernment, because Paul was clear that the rulers of his time did not discern

our Savior Jesus Christ, otherwise they would not have crucified the Lord of Glory.

How often have we fallen into ditches of our own choice because we did not discern the people before us? Some of us have been swindled out of a large amount of money, wasted our time and energy, and fallen prey to people claiming to be believers, only to find out they just used us for our influence and money. Some of us have produced products that never went anywhere because we lacked the discernment to connect with the right people.

We have also heard of creative people whose inventions and ideas were stolen because they did not discern the people they made their partners. I am sure that many of us can relate to these situations.

I pray, like Solomon, to have the wisdom and discernment required for our assignment and purpose on earth, especially in this season.

May the Lord give it to you abundantly!

3. *Hidden wisdom of God* – This is not the wisdom of this world, but the wisdom for the mature that has been hidden and ordained before the ages for our glory. It is very important to understand that the hidden wisdom of God that Paul talks about here is for our glory. The word glory used here is from the Greek word *doxa*, which means having a divine quality and the unspoken manifestation of God. It pertains to someone's value, substance, and essence. The word *doxa* is equivalent to the Old Testament Hebrew word *kabo*, which denotes God's infinite and intrinsic value. J. Thayer said it is "…what evokes good opinion," i.e., something which has inherent or intrinsic value." We can write a whole book just on this!

God has prepared hidden wisdom for our glory that will unlock our intrinsic and inherent value! We must come to a place where people see us as a wonder – a solution to someone's problem, an answer to someone in distress, and a light when someone is in darkness. Hence, living in the creative realm is vital because our creativity is our glory. This intrinsic and inherent value God has put in us needs to manifest for the world to experience and enjoy.

The revealer of God's hidden wisdom

According to 1 Corinthians 2:9, *"But as it is written: Eye has not seen, nor ear heard, nor have entered into the heart of man. The things which God has prepared for those who love Him."*

I believe Paul is also referring to our Book of Destiny in Psalm 139:16, where the Psalmist poetically states that our days are already "written" before there were any: *"Your eyes saw my substance, being yet unformed. And in Your book they all were written, The days fashioned for me, When as yet there were none of them."*

Apostle Paul is saying there are things, or hidden wisdom written about us that no eye has seen or ear heard, nor even entered into the heart of men. That is profound because it means that our parents, siblings, friends, relatives, church members, business associates, government officials, or even we ourselves have not seen or heard, nor has it entered into our hearts what God has prepared for us who love Him!

I don't know about you, but I am very excited to know God has planned for me what I haven't seen or heard and what I haven't even thought of. His plan, or blueprint of our existence, includes the creativity He has deposited in us. Two big questions arise:

> What creativity is in us that we have not seen,
> heard, or even thought of?

> How do we find it?

I believe the answer is in the following verses:

> But God has revealed them to us through His Spirit. For the Spirit searches all things, yes, the deep things of God. For what man knows the things of a man except the spirit of the man which is in him? Even so no one knows the things of God except the Spirit of God. Now we have received, not the spirit of the world, but the Spirit who is from God, that we might know the things that have been freely given to us by God.
> *(1 Corinthians 2:10-12)*

In the above verses Paul says God revealed these things to us through His Spirit.

What are these things?

They are the hidden wisdom about us that is in God. Paul said that no man knows the things in a man except the spirit of the man. Therefore no one knows what is in you and me except the spirit in us.

What's more, no one knows the things in God except the Spirit from Him. The Holy Spirit is the only One mandated by God to search all things. He diligently examines and searches all, again, *all* things and, yes, even the deep things of God. Thus, the Holy Spirit is responsible for revealing, uncovering, and bringing to light these mysteries that He has concealed before time for our glory. He is God's CIA – the intelligence behind everything in God's mind and heart. The hidden wisdom spoken in mysteries about us is therefore only revealed through us by the Spirit of God. He is the key to achieving the wisdom that we need to activate the creativity God has deposited in us! The good news is, once it is revealed, it now belongs to us!

Check out this principle in Deuteronomy 29:29, *"The secret things belong unto the Lord our God: but those things which are revealed belong unto* us and to our children forever, that we may do all the words of this law."* I can guarantee you, this is a promise we can take to the bank!

The other part of this promise of the Holy Spirit is found in verse 12: *"Now we have received, not the spirit of the world, but the Spirit who is from God, that we might know the things that have been freely given to us by God."* God has mandated the Holy Spirit to reveal the hidden wisdom in God so we can discover the things that have been freely given to us by God.

You cannot put any monetary value on this. Hidden wisdom was given to us for *free*. He *freely* gave it, not based on the merit of our actions, but because God's favor was bestowed upon us.

I pray and declare the hidden wisdom and the creativity that was freely given to you to manifest now!

Types of wisdom

> These things we also speak, not in words which man's wisdom teaches but which the Holy Spirit teaches, comparing spiritual things with spiritual. But the natural man does not receive the things of the Spirit of God, for they are foolishness to him; nor can he know them, because they are spiritually discerned. But he who is spiritual judges all things, yet he himself is rightly judged by no one. For "who has known the mind of the Lord that he may instruct Him?" But we have the mind of Christ.
>
> *(1 Corinthians 2:6-16)*

Then in 1 Corinthians 2:13, Paul introduced us to two types of wisdom teachers who teach in words versus spiritual things when he said, *"These things we also speak, not in words which man's wisdom teaches but which the Holy Spirit teaches, comparing spiritual things with spiritual."*

1. **Wisdom taught by the Holy Spirit** – The Holy Spirit living in us is the greatest teacher of spiritual things here on earth. That is

why I cannot stress enough the importance of having fellowship with the Holy Spirit. We have to come to the place of entering a new dimension of creativity, and it is by the Holy Spirit that we can do that. According to Ezekiel 2:1-2: *"And He said to me, 'Son of man, stand on your feet, and I will speak to you. Then the Spirit entered me when He spoke to me, and set me on my feet; and I heard Him who spoke to me 'Then the Spirit entered me when He spoke to me, and set me on my feet; and I heard Him who spoke to me.'"*

The Spirit did not just impart. He entered Ezekiel, which means He came and invaded every area of his life. Notice the consequence of Ezekiel's encounter with the greatest teacher on earth. Since this book is about living in the creative realm, I will expand the encounter from that angle.

A. *The Holy Spirit entered Ezekiel* – The Holy Spirit, who is the Spirit of Creativity, entered Him and invaded his physical being.

B. *He spoke to him* – Ezekiel heard the voice of the Holy Spirit.

C. *He set him on his feet* – According to freedictionary.com, *set on his feet* means to help one stand upright after being on the ground, and to restore one to a stable position after a downturn or misfortune.

That is very exciting! In our times of unproductivity, downturn, and misfortune – those times of our life when we cannot create or be creative, the Holy Spirit is the One who can stabilize and set us back on our feet to become productive again and create for the advancement of His Kingdom.

I pray you are reestablished again to produce what God created you to do.

D. *Ezekiel heard the Holy Spirit speak to him* – Ezekiel heard the instruction from the Spirit of the Living God. This dimension of the Spirit takes our hearing to another level. There are times I can't figure out how to create when I am given an idea, but when the Holy Spirit speaks and instructs me clearly how to do it, I'm the first one to be surprised by the creativity that flows through me after He speaks.

2. **Wisdom taught by man** – This "wisdom" is information and head knowledge without godly application, anointing, and inspiration by the Holy Spirit. It might look good to the world, but it amounts to nothing in the Kingdom. An example I can give is of two singers on the same stage: one taught by man, is a professionally trained singer with the best musicians and most expensive musical instruments – a performance the world applauds, versus someone who sings with the anointing of the Spirit, takes us into a higher dimension in God and inspires us to bow down before the Lord to worship Him in Spirit and Truth. By the time we get up, we are healed!

The Craftsman of all craftsmen

> I, wisdom, dwell with prudence and find out knowledge of witty inventions.
>
> *(Proverbs 8:12, KJV)*

> The Lord possessed me at the beginning of His way, Before His works of old. I have been established from everlasting, From the beginning, before there was ever an earth.
>
> *(Proverbs 8:22-23)*

> Then I was beside Him as a master craftsman; And I was daily His delight, Rejoicing always before Him. Rejoicing in His inhabited world, And my delight was with the sons of men.
>
> *(Proverbs 8:30-31)*

According to Matt Emerson:

> While Proverbs certainly gives us wisdom about day-to-day life, the early church read it primarily as a book about Wisdom himself—the Lord Jesus. This was especially true of Proverbs 8:22–31, one of the most important texts for the early church's understanding of Jesus. While there are plenty of exegetical arguments about these verses in the early church, almost everyone agreed that Lady Wisdom is a figurative depiction of God the Son. This is because other biblical texts identify Jesus as God's Wisdom, most importantly 1 Corinthians 1:24, where Paul calls Jesus, "Christ the power of God and the wisdom of God" (cf. Rev. 3:14; Prov. 8:22, 25). To put it simply, if Jesus is God's Wisdom, then Proverbs 8 must be a reference to Jesus since it refers to God's wisdom.[3]

In addition to what Matt said, we also find in Proverbs 8:6-8 that wisdom's words do not contain words of wickedness. Instead, they declare right and excellent things, truth and righteousness. And Jesus is the Word, and He is the only One who qualifies as the Word to hold these attributes, *"Listen, for I will speak of excellent things, And from the opening of my lips will come right things; For my mouth will speak truth; Wickedness is an abomination to my lips. All the words of my mouth are with righteousness."*

The revelations of Apostle John and Apostle Paul also confirm what the Psalmist said,

Our Innate Wisdom

> In the beginning was the Word, and the Word was with God, and the Word was God. He was in the beginning with God. All things were made through Him, and without Him nothing was made that was made" (John 1:1-3); "but to those who are called, both Jews and Greeks, Christ the power of God and the wisdom of God.
>
> *(1 Corinthians 2:24)*

We also find that wisdom personified is indeed the Master Craftsman. He was there before the foundation of the earth, He was beside God as a Master Craftsman, and He is the One that finds out knowledge of witty inventions. Witty inventions are creative ideas from the Lord that turn into inventions and can serve as a blessing to others to advance the Kingdom.

How then can we possibly create without wisdom, the Master Craftsman, with us? He is the finder of witty inventions we need in order to manifest our God-given assignment. Everything needs to be made through Him because He is the one that holds the realm of creative ideas and inventions. He is God's wisdom, and His delight is in the sons of men. We are His delight! That is our portion and our inheritance. Wisdom is looking forward for us to create, and to create continuously with Him.

> Now therefore, listen to me, my children,
> For blessed are those who keep my ways.
> Hear instruction and be wise,
> And do not disdain it.
> Blessed is the man who listens to me,
> Watching daily at my gates,
> Waiting at the posts of my doors.
> For whoever finds me finds life,
> And obtains favor from the Lord;

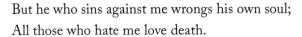

> But he who sins against me wrongs his own soul;
> All those who hate me love death.
>
> *(Proverbs 8:32-36)*

I want to end with the last verses of Proverbs 8 above. Verse 34 shows us the attributes of those who are called to live in the creative realm – in the realm of ability:

a. *To listen* – We must listen to make sure that we are hearing His instructions and that they align with His ways. Our God-given creative ideas must be produced.

b. *To watch at His gates* – We cannot afford to sleep and miss His instructions. We must be awake and watch to perform what we were instructed to do. Gates of opportunity open at certain times. We can't miss the opportunity to enter because we have been caught sleeping!

c. *To wait at the posts of His doors* – Waiting is a must. Haste makes waste. Timing is critical in the Kingdom of God. Just because we have an idea doesn't mean we need to create it immediately. There is wisdom in waiting – a period of preparation, planning and counting the cost before we venture into something. We have to lay a proper foundation so that when the door finally opens, we are ready, and all our efforts will not go to waste.

If we hear His instructions and do not disdain them, watch at the gates and wait at His doors, we will inherit a corresponding promise for abiding by these attributes in accordance to verse 36 as follows:

- We will be blessed
- We will find life
- We will obtain favor from the Lord

And if we don't:

- We will wrong our own souls and
- it will lead to death!

Knowing Jesus as the wisdom of God helps us navigate our day-to-day life differently. I therefore encourage you to seek wisdom, listen to Him, and follow His ways so that you might find favor in His sight.

Prayer of Release #6
– Our Innate God-Given Wisdom

Supernatural Decrees for Breakthrough

The Word says in Job 22:28, "decree a thing and it shall be established," therefore,

- I acknowledge that I cannot do anything without God's wisdom.

- I decree and declare that I have abundant and generous wisdom to perform the assignments God has given me. My creativity has all the wisdom it requires to fulfill God's purpose through me.

- I decree and declare that I have God's perfect timing. I do not hasten to make things work. I listen for His instructions, watch at the gates and wait at the posts of His doors until I have clear understanding of what He wants me to do.

- I decree and declare that I see my blueprints that are hidden in God's mind because I have the Holy Spirit, who is the Revealer of Mysteries. He searches all things about me that are in God's heart.

- I decree and declare that I am taught by the Holy Spirit and not by man, or the ruler of this age whose wisdom has no discernment and comes to nothing.

- I decree and declare that I listen to His instructions and therefore find life, am blessed, and find favor in His sight.

LIFE APPLICATION SECTION

Memory Verse

Then I was beside Him as a master craftsman; And I was daily His delight, Rejoicing always before Him. Rejoicing in His inhabited world, And my delight was with the sons of men. *(Proverbs 8:30-31)*

Reflections

1. What are the benefits of following God's instructions?

2. Why is it important to have divine wisdom to live in the creative realm?

CHAPTER 7

YOU ARE GOD'S MASTERPIECE; A WALKING PIECE OF ART

> For we are His workmanship [His own master work, a work of art], created in Christ Jesus [reborn from above – spiritually transformed, renewed, ready to be used] for good works, which God prepared [for us] beforehand [taking paths which He set], so that we would walk in them [living the good life which He prearranged and made ready for us].
>
> *(Ephesians 2:10, Amp)*

> Painting is poetry that is seen rather than felt, and poetry is a painting that is felt rather than seen.
>
> *(Leonardo Da Vinci)*

The first phrase of Ephesians 2:10 reads, "For we are God's handiwork" (NIV). Other translations state that we are God's "accomplishment" (CEB), "workmanship" (ESV, KJV), or "masterpiece" (NLT). Masterpiece or workmanship is from the Greek word *poiema*, which is related etymologically to the word poem. But *poiema*, is also related to the verb *poieo* (to make).

We are God's masterpiece! Since we are His masterpiece, the work of Picasso, Rembrandt, and the best artist you will find on earth cannot be compared to us, *His* masterpiece!

You are God's Masterpiece; a Walking Piece of Art

Many believers suffer from the sin of comparison and the lie coming from the spirit of unworthiness. I remember a story of a beautiful young woman from one of Francis' healing meetings. This woman was on the verge of suicide with drugs because she thought she was ugly. That is one of the enemy's schemes to sabotage and paralyze our walk. I know of people who will not come out of their house because they have zits on their faces. Did that ever happen to you? I used to do that!

Before I came to the Lord I did not like how I looked. I did not like that I was born an Asian with an accent. There were times I tried to conceal my accent by trying to sound American. After I got delivered, I became conscious of the beauty God has given me. In addition, people started telling me how much they liked my accent! The enemy certainly had a field day during the time I bought his lies.

Praise God for the saving grace of the Lord Jesus Christ and the healing that I have experienced as I started walking with Him. Now, I am confident in my appearance and communications. I don't compare myself to others because of my confidence in God's handiwork. I am His artwork – a display of His excellence that deserves to be in an art gallery (treasured) for others to appreciate. I am not worried about how others see me. I am secure in the way God created me. I have peace, and I love the way I look!

I just read about a woman who paid a lot of money to have work done to her face. The left side of her face became paralyzed and deformed due to complications from the surgery.

> When will it end?

The answer is, when we finally realize that we are His masterpiece!

Art defined

The *Amplified* version of Ephesians 3:20 refers to us as a "work of art," so let me define what art means. The etymology of the term "art" is related to the Latin word "ars," meaning art, skill, or craft. According to *Oxford Dictionary*, art is the expression or application of human creative skill and imagination, typically in a visual form such as painting or sculpture, producing works to be appreciated primarily for their beauty or emotional power. *Merriam-Webster Dictionary* defines art as something created with imagination and skill, beautiful, or that expresses important ideas or feelings.

We have been created, imagined, and carefully thought through by our Divine Creator. No human being can match, or compete with His creativity! God expressed His creative skills through us. He created us with a beauty that cannot be reproduced. We are one of a kind. The way we walk, our facial expressions, the way we move our hands when we talk, and every move we make is an expression of God's creativity.

We are indeed a piece of art – a canvas that first existed in the mind of God, now manifested as poetry here on earth.

Poetry consists of stanzas. Acclaimed poet and former USA Poet Laureate Billy Collins says:

> In poetry, a stanza is used to describe the main building block of a poem. It is a unit of poetry composed of lines that relate to a similar thought or topic – like a paragraph in prose or a verse in a song. Every stanza in a poem has its own concept and serves a unique purpose. In Italian, the word "stanza" means "room." Stanzas then function in a poem like rooms function in a house "You're taking the reader on a tour of the poem, room by room, like taking someone through your house and describing it." In this way, stanzas can be particularly revealing: the structure of a poem's stanzas says a lot about the poem, just as the rooms in a house say a lot about the house.[4]

God is the Master Poet, and we are His poem. Our life is poetry full of stanzas that reveal God's handiwork in every aspect declaring His unique purpose for each room of our lives. Every move we make should therefore be a declaration of His poetic utterance about our lives. Our lives should be like a tour portraying the different facets of every room God wants to show off about us.

Our lives are a poetic utterance of the Master Poet. I don't know about you, but I am excited just at the thought that I am a walking piece of art manifesting as His poem!

We are created in Christ Jesus

We are created in Christ Jesus. Created here is from the Greek word, *ktízō*, which means to build and create and only applies to God who alone can make what was "not there before."

That is very profound if we think about it. Our designer is not from this world, but is the Only One and True God, our Maker, our Creator who is not human, but Divine. And He created us in Christ Jesus, that according to the *Amplified* version means, "as *reborn from above—spiritually transformed, renewed, ready to be used.*" As New Testament believers, it is life-changing to understand that our creative skills have now been renewed and transformed through Christ. They are now activated. We are ready to go and be used as we live in the creative realm.

Our paths have been set

Our lives should never be boring. Boredom occurs when we are not doing anything, or when our untapped passion trapped within us is not activated in our ecosystem.

I have good news for you.

A boring life should never be our portion because God has already set our path. Our direction and destination have been prearranged, put together, and made ready. All we need is to walk in them! And part of that is to live a good life.

I was driving in Oregon with our friends, passing through the mountains to go to a farm in California. I could see the genius of the engineers who planned, created and paved the road through this treacherous terrain. On the other side were miles and miles of streams of water. The thought of how they bulldozed through the mountains without disturbing the streams of water fascinated me.

And here we are. The road has already been paved before us! It was prearranged before we even existed. All we need is to see the road and walk on it. Wow!

The consciousness of being a piece of art should give us peace and rest to live a good life. Part of our beauty as God's masterpiece is the ability to live in the creative realm and access God's creativity to show the world His handiwork. People do not flock to stadiums to see a basketball player who cannot score a game; they don't line up for hours to spend money on a new computer that doesn't increase productivity; they don't visit galleries of horrible art that is displeasing to the eyes; nor do they eat food at restaurants that is not appetizing. People are drawn to good things. They are willing to spend time, energy, and money when something is produced with excellence. That is what our lives should reflect – a masterpiece of a good life!

His creative seed

Paul told the Ephesians that we were created as a masterpiece in Christ Jesus prepared to perform good deeds to accomplish what He has ordained for us to do.

We are created to perform good deeds. Period. God created all things, including man, to reproduce after their own kind. We therefore know when someone is not performing a good deed – they are not reproducing. This is a law according to Genesis 1:11: *"Then God said, 'Let the earth bring forth grass, the herb that yields seed, and the fruit tree that yields fruit according to its kind, whose seed is in itself, on the earth,' and it was so."*

In this verse, we find that God's creation includes seeds that yield seeds of their own kind. That means if you plant a mango seed, it will not produce a peach tree. Similarly, a cat will not give birth to a dog. We are seeds that have to produce our own kind. I believe that if we look at ourselves as seeds, we will approach our life differently.

As seeds, we are subject to the seasons and timing of God. We see this in Genesis 8:22: *"While the earth remains, Seedtime and harvest, Cold and heat, Winter and summer, And day and night Shall not cease."* Since we are talking about living in the creative realm, based on this passage we have to look at some of our time spent planting creative seeds. Each seed represents a stanza, or a room that God has to build through us as He takes others on a tour of our house, or life.

As creative seeds, we also have time to plant and harvest. We must be careful of where we plant ourselves and of the timing. Therefore, to harvest a creative idea, you must plant a seed of creativity. The world must see the ending of His poem, our life – a poem that must be finished and end well.

No excuse

You will never see anywhere in the Bible where it mentions God creating tables and chairs. Our houses are hidden inside the trees that He created for us to use as materials to produce them.

Similarly, God never created cars and plastic. The cars are hidden in the earth through minerals that combine iron with other elements. Then when the carbon content of iron is reduced, steel is produced. Crude oil and natural gas are used to make plastics (produced by combining ethane from natural gas and propane from crude oil). The process of making cars and plastic is more complicated than what I am sharing here, but I want you to see that God created the materials, but gave men the intelligence to come up with creative ideas to produce things on earth from the resources He has provided. As a result, there is no excuse for us New Testament believers to be poor. Poverty is not about a lack of money; it is simply a lack of productivity and seeds (creative ideas) to produce a product.

> *I pray your creative seeds emerge, that you plant them in due season and harvest them at His appointed time, so the world can tour every room in your house where you show off God's craftsmanship through you! May you never forget, you are God's Masterpiece!*

Prayer of Release #7
– You are God's Masterpiece

Supernatural Decrees for Breakthrough

The Word says in Job 22:28, "decree a thing and it shall be established," therefore,

- I decree and declare that God is my Creator. I am designed by a Divine Being. I am unique, one of a kind, created for His glory. I do not allow the spirit of comparison to operate in my life because I am secure in the One who designed me. I am His masterpiece.

- I decree and declare that I am God's poetry – a walking scroll of psalms. My life is a poem, and I conduct my life as such. I create my stanzas and rooms for the world to explore to see His beauty and glory.

- I decree and declare that I am spiritually transformed, renewed, and ready to be used. I am His piece of art.

- I decree and declare that I have no excuse not to create and to be poor. Everything has already been provided for me. I just need God's wisdom to give me the creative idea of what He needs me to produce.

- I decree and declare that I no longer allow boredom to overwhelm me. A boring life will never be my portion because God has already set up my path.

LIFE APPLICATION SECTION

Memory Verse

For we are His workmanship [His own master work, a work of art], created in Christ Jesus [reborn from above—spiritually transformed, renewed, ready to be used] for good works, which God prepared [for us] beforehand [taking paths which He set], so that we would walk in them [living the good life which He prearranged and made ready for us]. *(Ephesians 2:10, AMP)*

Reflections

1. What do you mean by workmanship?
   _____
   _____
   _____
   _____
   _____

2. What are the creative seeds that God put in you?
   _____
   _____
   _____
   _____
   _____

CHAPTER 8

DETOX YOUR MIND!

> For as he thinks in his heart, so is he. "Eat and drink!" he says to you, but his heart is not with you.
>
> *(Proverbs 23:7)*

> It doesn't matter where you come from, what you have or don't have, what you lack, or what you have too much of. But all you need to have is faith in God, an undying passion for what you do and what you choose to do in this life, and a relentless drive and the will to do whatever it takes to be successful in whatever you put your mind to.
>
> *(Stephen Curry)*

Another key to living in the creative realm is to have a sound mind and to be aligned with the Mind of all minds – *the Mind of Christ*. Everything is built twice: it first exists in the spiritual realm through the mind of God, then it is created in the natural realm by those who partner with Him on earth. I always say, if we see it, we can manifest it. Thus, partnering with the Holy Spirit and the Wisdom of God is key to seeing what God has already put in us.

Remember Mary Lou Retton, the Olympic Gold Medalist?

Living in the Creative Realm

About six weeks before the games were to start, Retton suffered a major knee injury, which turned out to be torn cartilage. She and her parents opted for minimally invasive arthroscopic surgery, which enabled Retton to walk immediately and to begin training after just one week of physical therapy. In the weeks before the Games, Retton would lie in bed, her eyes closed, imagining each piece of equipment and each routine and performing perfectly. Then she imagined receiving the gold medal with "The Star-Spangled Banner" booming around her.[5]

Finally the day arrived. I will never forget it. Most of the TVs in America were tuned in during the Olympic Games in 1984. America watched as she stood at the end of the mat and prepared for her final vault. We held our breath in anticipation of her performance, because she needed a perfect score of 10 to take home the Olympic gold. She closed her eyes for a moment as she positioned herself, broke into a full sprint and scored a perfect 10. Her performance earned her and her Team USA gold medals around their necks! A reporter then asked her what was going through her mind when she closed her eyes before sprinting. She told them she saw herself executing every move precisely and flawlessly to achieve a perfect score.

That is the work of a righteous mind, and that is what we need. But unrighteous things can similarly be built by partnering with the demonic realm. Our creativity is then used for the kingdom of darkness instead of the Kingdom of Light. The songs we compose, the books we write, paintings we paint, and inventions we make can shift our followers' minds toward God, or against Him.

We can limit God!

A mind that is not conformed to the Mind of Christ can hinder our creativity. Many of us are unaware that we can limit God, thus preventing His creativity from freely flowing through us. What a terrifying thought! There is actually a Scripture to prove this statement. According to Psalm 78:41, *"Yes, again and again they tempted God, and limited the Holy One of Israel."* How can a God of the impossible with infinite possibilities and power be limited? In Psalm 78, Asaph, the Psalmist, chronicled the history of the walk of the Israelites from the splitting of the Red Sea so they could pass through it; to provision of manna in the desert so they would not die of starvation; to safe guidance into the Holy Land by driving out their enemies; to possession of their Promised Land. After all He did, they continued to tempt and provoke Him through unbelief and unfaithfulness:

- Psalm 78:19: *"Yes, they spoke against God: They said, 'Can God prepare a table in the wilderness?'"*

- Psalm 78:36: *"Nevertheless they flattered Him with their mouth, And they lied to Him with their tongue.*

- Psalm 78:58: *"For they provoked Him to anger with their high places, And moved Him to jealousy with their carved images."*

All this from not having the Mind of Christ!

According to Google, the mind is the element of a person that enables them to be aware of the world and their experiences: to think and to feel, the faculty of consciousness and thought. Consciousness is the state of being awake and aware of one's surroundings. A thought is the action or process of thinking; it is an idea or opinion produced by thinking or occurring suddenly in the mind.

The statement "occurring suddenly in the mind" is significant because most people think all their thoughts are their own. Far from the truth!

Every day we have thoughts occurring in our mind, some of which I call random, or trajectory thoughts. For me these are thoughts that suddenly come when I am not even thinking about them. I can be driving, and suddenly I think, *You left the iron on*, or, *You did not lock the door!* Then worry comes, and I find myself turning around to go back to my house only to discover my door was locked and the iron unplugged. What a waste of time! Did that ever happen to you? With these notes I will give you five different sources of thought.

1. **Positive and righteous thoughts**

    These thoughts come from the Kingdom of God, and produce the nine fruits of the Spirit:

    - Love
    - Joy
    - Peace
    - Longsuffering
    - Kindness
    - Goodness
    - Faithfulness
    - Gentleness
    - Self- Control

If these fruits are not present, you can take it to the bank that your thoughts are not coming from the realm of righteousness, because they don't align with the Mind of Christ, His will, or His purpose for your life.

2. **Negative and unrighteous thoughts**

    These thoughts come from the kingdom of darkness (i.e., gossip, offense, unforgiveness, betrayal, sexual perversion, lies, manipulation, bribery, and the list goes on). They produce thoughts that bring forth sickness, failure, stagnation, and eventually physical or spiritual death.

3. **Natural thoughts**

    We need these thoughts for performing our routine day-to-day tasks and activities, like taking a bath, eating three meals a day, cleaning the house, and so on. They result from our awareness of our environment and the world we live in, the current temperature of the day as being hot or cold, and more. For example: *It is raining outside, so I need an umbrella.*

4. **Thoughts influenced by people surrounding us**

    These thoughts are influenced by information from our family, friends, the news, social media, and colleagues. They affect our decision-making. That is why we need to surround ourselves with people who are our destiny helpers instead of destiny robbers.

5. **Wasted thoughts**

    These are filler thoughts. They deserve to be in the trash can because they lack spiritual or lasting value. I call them the blah, blah, blah of the mind.

James 1:12-16 gives us the stages how our thoughts manifest from the spiritual realm into the natural realm:

> Blessed is the man who endures temptation; for when he has been approved, he will receive the crown of life which the Lord has promised to those who love Him. Let no one say

when he is tempted, "I am tempted by God"; for God cannot be tempted by evil, nor does He Himself tempt anyone. But each one is tempted when he is drawn away by his own desires and enticed. Then, when desire has conceived, it gives birth to sin; and sin, when it is full-grown, brings forth death.

James is very clear: temptation doesn't come from God. It is up to us to endure temptations and nip them in the bud. Endurance shows our love for Him, and God promises we will receive the crown of life in return. The crown of life is a reward – an honor that our Lord Jesus bestows on us for faithfully persevering and enduring temptations, trials, and tribulations.

Dear Saint: purpose in your heart to receive the crown of life!

Stages of thinking

The Bible states that we perish for lack of knowledge, so let's examine what James said in the above passages.

I pray this revelation from the Holy Spirit helps the Body of Christ endure temptations from the enemy, so we don't fall into the enemy's trap and so we avoid the latter part of what I call the "stages of thinking" as follows:

1. **A thought or Idea –** *"But each one is tempted."*

    The problem starts when the enemy tempts us with a thought or an idea. A single man or woman is introduced to their married boss, a beautiful woman, or a gorgeous man. Then a thought comes to them: *Wow, she's a beautiful woman; she looks like a model*, or *He is such a muscular and a good-looking man!* This is the first stage, and it is a normal thought. It happens all the time. Our eyes love beauty, and there is nothing wrong with admiring a beautiful person or thing.

2. **Imagination** – *"When he is drawn away."*

This is when someone starts to imagine and chew on the thought instead of just letting it go, or spitting it out like a rotten apple. Based on the previous scenario, that person can continue the thought by imagining what it would be like to be in the arms of their boss while they watch a movie together. That is when we need to nip these thoughts in the bud immediately. There is no reason to even think about being with a married man or woman.

3. **Desire** – *"by his own desires and enticed."*

This is the stage of obsession. I call it the danger zone; it is no longer just a thought. The thought now becomes a desire to be with this person. It goes from the conscious mind into the subconscious mind where the thought becomes a part of us. It is like driving a car. Once we learn to drive, it becomes automatic. We don't have to think hard about which pedal to press to move or stop the car. Similarly, the beautiful person is now a part of their daily routine; they wake up thinking about them and go to bed with their image in their head.

Gotcha!

That's a hollow word of victory and it sounds like a clanging cymbal in the spiritual realm. The demons are having a party! The person is now lured or hooked by his temptation – entangled and trapped like an animal in a net hanging on a tree.

4. **Conception** – *"when desire has conceived."*

The person ends up having an extramarital affair and conceives an unrighteous seed. She is pregnant! This needs no further explanation at this stage except that the unrighteous seed is ready to be birthed. Even if the person involved wants to abort it, the action has already been taken.

5. **Manifestation** – *"it gives birth to sin."*
   Sin has been birthed as a consequence of an immoral act against the divine law of righteousness. We can now relate to what happened to Adam and Eve when they partook of the fruit from the tree of the knowledge of good and evil. Their sin cost them the presence of God. They were taken out of the garden – out of His presence!

6. **End result** – *"and sin when it is full-grown, brings forth death."*
   Death! God helps us! My prayer is for this stage never to manifest in our lives.
   I decree and declare that you will purposely choose the blessing of the endurance of temptation that James declared upon you instead of the death it brings: "Blessed is the man who endures temptation; for when he has been approved, he will receive the crown of life which the Lord has promised to those who love Him." *I decree and declare for you to receive the crown of life that our Lord Jesus Christ bestows on you as He honors those who faithfully serve Him and remain steadfast in their journey, whether in a storm, or not. May this be your portion, in Jesus' Mighty Name!*

The battle of the mind

Have you ever wondered why there are so many books and sermons titled, *The Battle of the Mind*? Because that is precisely what it is!

We are constantly at war, and the enemy uses our minds as a landing strip for his thoughts of temptation. We are continually bombarded with thoughts from the kingdom of darkness to weaken us with the hope that one day we will succumb to his temptations. We must therefore become strong-minded for His Kingdom. We need to understand that we are not at war with the flesh, but with invisible forces that are against the knowledge of God, as stated in 2 Corinthians 10:3-6:

> For though we walk in the flesh, we do not war according to the flesh. For the weapons of our warfare are not carnal but mighty in God for pulling down strongholds, casting down arguments and every high thing that exalts itself against the knowledge of God, bringing every thought into captivity to the obedience of Christ, and being ready to punish all disobedience when your obedience is fulfilled.

Both the Kingdom of Light and darkness begin with a mindset and aim to fortify our minds to form strongholds. It is up to us which type of stronghold we accept in our life.

A mindset, according to *Merriam-Webster Dictionary*, is a mental attitude or inclination; it is a fixed state of mind. According to *Oxford Dictionary*, "a stronghold is a place that has been fortified to protect it against attack; it is also a place where a particular cause or belief is strongly defended or upheld." A mindset becomes a stronghold when you allow demonic thoughts to be fortified forming a wall of defense around a thinking pattern to compel you always to think that way.

How mindsets are formed

1. **Culture** – Culture is a way of life of a people group, a region, or nation. We come from different backgrounds that help mold our perceptions, beliefs, lives, marriages, and relationships. Culture can be expressed through language, arts, skills, literature, philosophy, religion, music, customs, traditions, and ways of doing business. It is simply a template for our worldview. For instance, some nations require a dowry from the groom before their parents and elders can agree to the marriage. So, if a Western groom marries a bride from one of these nations, it would be dishonorable to the family if he doesn't bring a dowry. In other cultures the parents are responsible for finding their daughter's

husband. All I can do right now is praise God that I am not from that culture!

2. **Past experiences** – A mindset is also built as a result of an experience, bad or good. A woman who has been sexually traumatized could end up hating men, resulting in her emotions and love turning toward another woman. One of the common denominators in the lives of homosexuals and lesbians is molestation and sexual abuse, resulting in gender confusion.

3. **Education** – Mindsets are formed through education. We need to study and go to institutions whose teachings are based on the biblical ideology of the Kingdom. In this generation we see so many parents homeschooling because of the continuous erosion of our education system, in which the mindset of our children is being molded to think atheistically without the knowledge of God. Currently, here in the United States, parents are in an uproar because their children are being taught and confused by transgenderism and satanic manuals are even being allowed in schools.

   We truly need to ensure that our children, and the children of the next generation – the future leaders of our country – are brought up in the ways of the Kingdom as in Proverbs 22:6: *"Train up a child in the way he should go, And when he is old he will not depart from it."*

4. **Level of exposure** – One's success in life, ministry, business, and church is determined by one's level of exposure to various teachings, cultures of countries visited, and interactions with people of influence, as well as society around one. I know of churches built in excellence because they have been exposed to other ministries. I am not sure where I would be now if I still lived in the Philippines.

Detox your Mind!

According to Proverbs 23:7, *"As a man thinketh so is he."* Proverbs didn't say, As a man thinketh so he shall be.

Consider this: if we think depression, we are already depressed; if we think unworthiness, we are already unworthy. The exciting news is that these mindsets can be unlearned and reprogrammed so we can prove what is the good, acceptable, and perfect will of God. Apostle Paul requested earnestly in Romans 12:2:

> I beseech you therefore, brethren, by the mercies of God, that you present your bodies a living sacrifice, holy, acceptable to God, which is your reasonable service. And do not be conformed to this world, but be transformed by the renewing of your mind, that you may prove what is that good and acceptable and perfect will of God.

Apostle Paul described the three types of minds in Romans 12:2:

1. **Conformed mind** – The attitude of this type of mind is, In the beginning there was me, myself and I. Everything done with this mind will never align with the will of God. It is a mind that strives to create something, or makes things happen out of its own will and volition. The word conform is from the Greek word, *suschématizó*, which means to assume a particular form or pattern; or to fashion oneself to a certain figure. It is likened to water that assumes the shape or form of any container into which it is poured. Paul implored the Romans not to be conformed to the world, or not to copy the behavior and customs of the world. We are required to be "In the world, but not of it," because the world consists of the things that reject God and everything He represents.

    Many believers blend well with the world by adopting their unrighteous ideologies and way of living. It is no longer uncommon to read news of pastors and bishops caught in adultery, sex trafficking, and driving while intoxicated. Lack of reverence for the things of God has reduced their lifestyles to the world's standards. They should instead be aligned with the standards of God's Word.

2. **Transformed mind** – Transform is from the Greek word *metamorphoó*, which means to transfigure. To be transfigured is to be changed into another form, like what happened to Jesus in Matthew 17:2; *"...and He was transfigured before them. His face shone like the sun, and His clothes became as white as the light."*

3. **Renewed mind** – Renewal of the mind occurs when one experiences a complete change of heart and life by allowing the Holy Spirit to change the way they think. Renewed thinking starts with what I call "in the beginning-God!" Thus the beginning of our life starts with God: our marriage, the way we rear our children, our career, and our relationships, they all begin with God. When He is the center of everything we do, we can never doubt that the end result aligns with His will, producing and birthing His purpose for our lives.

The Mind of Christ

A person's conformed mind must experience a metamorphosis. It happens when they allow their mind to be transformed into the "pattern Mind" – the mind we have when we allow the Holy Spirit to renew it and change the way we think. Paul discovered this Mind when he said in Philippians 2:5, *"Let this mind be in you which was also in Christ Jesus."* What kind of a Mind was in Christ Jesus? It is found in the subsequent verses:

> ...who, being in the form of God, did not consider it robbery to be equal with God, but made Himself of no reputation,

taking the form of a bondservant, and coming in the likeness of men. And being found in appearance as a man, He humbled Himself and became obedient to the point of death, even the death of the cross. Therefore God also has highly exalted Him and given Him the name which is above every name, that at the name of Jesus every knee should bow, of those in heaven, and of those on earth, and of those under the earth, and that every tongue should confess that Jesus Christ is Lord, to the glory of God the Father.

(Philippians 2:6-11)

1. **A mind of no reputation** – Jesus took the form of a bondservant and took the likeness and appearance of a man. Most of us fall into the sin of fearing man and therefore trying to save our reputation. We go out of our way to defend ourselves just to "save face" – avoid shame and humiliation. The hardest thing to do is to be quiet when arrows of accusations fly our way. Our initial instinct is to protect our reputation, at times at the expense of another person. Human nature always finds a scapegoat to avoid blame or exposure. I know, because I have done it myself.

2. **A humble mind** – Jesus humbled Himself. The most painful times of my life were during situations when I was in pride. Humility is the antidote to pride. It is one of the most potent weapons for diffusing one of the nemeses of the Kingdom of God. The sin of pride is the very reason why Lucifer fell and lost his position as the worship leader in the presence of God. I have seen people melt down from their high horses when the other party responded in humility instead of pride. Can you relate?

3. **An Obedient mind** – Jesus became obedient to the point of death, even the death on the Cross. Obedience to God's

instructions and commands sometimes results in death to our flesh.

Once when my husband was invited to preach, one of the pastor's wives shook everybody's hand except mine. I knew in my spirit that it was intentional, since it happened twice! We were invited to dinner after the meeting. My husband and I sat at a table where everyone could greet us before they went to the buffet. Of course, this woman was there. What did she do? She greeted my husband and completely ignored me. My pride kicked in, and smoke started wafting from my nose as I thought, *"Who the heck does she think she is ignoring me; I am the speaker's wife!"*

After a few hours, I saw them get up to leave. I heard a very authoritative voice say, *Get up and say goodbye to her.*

I reacted without hesitation. *What God? You've gotta be kidding me! No way, Jose!*

Then I heard, *Get up now!*

The fear of the Lord came upon me. I always fear possible consequences if I don't obey God. I hurriedly got up and walked toward the door to say goodbye to her. She was shocked to see me. I said, "I never had a chance to talk to you". I then hugged her and went back to the table.

The following day was the last day of the conference, and who do I see? The same woman! Again! I was so irritated! It was a Sunday, and I assumed they would be at their church. Then I heard the host pastor introduce me as the speaker's wife, and to my surprise, this woman did not just clap her hands, she stood up to honor me! That's when I learned the lesson of Proverbs 22:4: *"The reward of humility and the fear of the LORD are riches, honor, and life."*

The three departments of the mind and their importance

Understanding the correlation among the three departments of the mind is very important. It makes it easier to activate the creativity within us. This section could be another book in itself, and I cannot elaborate further in this book, but it is essential to know these principles to live in the creative realm. I encourage you, do your research to better understand this topic and to be more effective in having the Mind of Christ.

1. *The Conscious mind* – has also been called the human or carnal mind. It includes such things as sensations, perceptions, memories, feelings, and fantasies within our current awareness. According to *yourdictionary.com*, it is that part of mental activity during which one is fully aware at any given time. It is the awareness that something is happening and is the normal state of being awake. It is characterized by having an awareness of one's existence, sensations and thoughts. It is that part of the brain that gathers information and knowledge from our natural and physical environment through our five senses, like the awareness of the scent of a flower, the movement of a fish as it swims, the touch of wind blowing through one's hair, and the temperature of the water as we wade along the beach.

    The conscious mind's most incredible power is its ability to reason. It also can choose or reject. The reasoning part of our mind helps us choose the food we eat, the car we drive, the house we live in, and the partner we marry.

2. *The Subconscious mind* – Are you a dancer or a dance choreographer? Do you remember when you had to practice to perfect every movement required as you danced to the beat of a song? Are you a musician? Do you remember when you had to stay up late to play the piano, beat your drum and take the guitar

strings to another level? What about the first time you rode a bike?

We find that whatever we do, our first attempt is always the hardest. I remember learning to do things for the first time, be it riding a bike, driving a car, or creating digital arts. I was always conscious of every movement I made. My concentration and focus to accomplish my task were very high, but as I became skilled in driving, riding my bike, or creating digital arts, my awareness and consciousness of movements I was making became less. The effort I put into doing the tasks also became less because I did them without thinking. It became automatic.

These movements that are now automatic are driven and guided by one of the most potent forces in human behavior – the subconscious mind. The subconscious mind is that part of the mind that is not in a state of awareness. It is responsible for recording events in our lives that contain memories, whether bad or good, and emotions connected to them that produce thoughts, reactions, and habits. It significantly contributes to how we live and make decisions in our lives.

I once heard a story of a husband hugging his wife from behind while she was washing the dishes. She abruptly pushed him and yelled at him at the top of her voice. The husband was perplexed by her reaction to the love and affection he just showed her. It turned out that when she was a teenager, she had been sexually assaulted from behind. The husband's way of showing affection had triggered that event and the traumatic memory that caused her reaction.

It is imperative to protect your thoughts because the subconscious mind cannot determine between imagination and reality. That is why I cannot emphasize enough the importance of having the Mind of Christ. The subconscious mind is like fertile soil, and we are farmers. Whatever we plant will eventually harvest and eat, either bad fruit like discord, jealousy, hate, and unforgiveness, or good, if we plant peace, joy, love, and happiness. The sooner we change the way we think and replace our negative thoughts with positive, the sooner we will reap a better and more successful life and be more effective in living in the creative realm, according to the wisdom in Proverbs 4:23: *"Keep your heart with all diligence, For out of it spring the issues of life."*

3. *Superconscious mind* – Napoleon Hill, perhaps the most outstanding researcher on success in the 20th century, called superconsciousness "infinite intelligence." He spent 20 years interviewing at least 500 of the most successful men and women in America at that time. He concluded that without exception, they had tapped into this higher form of intelligence.

    I believe superconsciousness is the purest source of our creativity. It represents God's divine intelligence that is responsible for creating new ideas that have not been seen before. It is what Thomas Edison tapped into when he invented the light bulb, carbon telephone transmitter, and automatic telegraph. This God-given creative intelligence was also responsible for the discovery of the airplane by the Wright brothers.

    I am still in awe, trying to fathom how I can be transported through the air for 16 hours every time I'm on the plane traveling non-stop to South Africa. This invention alone proves there is an intelligence beyond our human mind, that if tapped into, results in creativity beyond our wildest imagination. This divine creativity changes the world and the way we live.

I pray and declare the Mind of Christ over us. Lord. We come before you by the Blood of Jesus and ask for permission to enter the Courts of Heaven right now to prosecute the altars in our mind that satan has planted in our bloodlines and our souls. In Jesus' name, we pray.

Heavenly Father, righteous judge, we acknowledge our guilt in these matters. We repent for anything we or our forefathers have done that opened the door to altars in our minds that control our God-given destinies. We ask that the Blood of Jesus speak for us now in the Courts by cleansing us from all sin and all legitimate accusations of satan. In Jesus' Name, we pray

We bring judgment in the Courts against evil altars that have delayed or stolen what is in our Book of Destiny. We receive supernatural grace to live on every page of our Book of Destiny.

So now I declare that the verdict has been granted!

Prayer of Release #8
– Detox Your Mind!

Supernatural Decrees for Breakthrough

The Word says in Job 22:28, "decree a thing and it shall be established," therefore,

- I decree and declare that I have a sound mind. The enemy can no longer occupy and dwell in my mind as if it were his real estate. I take back the keys to my mind, and refuse to give them to him. He will not enter again and create havoc by giving me thoughts from his dominion. I have the Mind of Christ.

- I decree and declare the Mind of Christ over me. I have a humble and obedient mind. It is my desire to have a mind of no reputation.

- I decree and declare that my mind is aligned with the Mind of Christ. My education, past experiences and traumas, my culture and social upbringing are no longer a hindrance to the mindset of the Kingdom.

- I decree and declare that I am blessed because I can endure temptation; I have been approved. I will receive the Crown of Life that the Lord has promised to those who love Him.

- I decree and declare that I have the discernment to recognize where my thoughts are coming from and the grace to nip in the bud every thought that is not of God so it cannot conceive and manifest. Sin that produces death is not my portion.

LIFE APPLICATION SECTION

Memory Verse

Blessed is the man who endures temptation; for when he has been approved, he will receive the crown of life which the Lord has promised to those who love Him. Let no one say when he is tempted, "I am tempted by God"; for God cannot be tempted by evil, nor does He Himself tempt anyone. But each one is tempted when he is drawn away by his own desires and enticed. Then, when desire has conceived, it gives birth to sin; and sin, when it is full-grown, brings forth death. *(James 1:12-16)*

Reflections

1. How are mindsets formed?

2. What are the Stages of Thinking?

CHAPTER 9

FEAR NOT!

For God has not given us a spirit of fear, but of power and of love and of a sound mind.

(2 Timothy 1:7)

Let me assert my firm belief that the only thing we have to fear is fear itself — nameless, unreasoning, unjustified terror which paralyzes needed efforts to convert retreat into advance.

(Franklin D. Roosevelt)

Fear is intrinsic to everything you do as a creative person. You're constantly putting yourself up there to be trashed. If I thought about it too much, I'd just be crippled. I'd rather create.

(Natalie Portman, Los Angeles Times, Oct 15, 2009)

One of the nemeses of creativity is fear. There are many Scriptures on *"fear not"* in the Bible for us to declare and apply to conquer it during our day-to-day life.

What is fear?

According to Google, *Fear* is "an unpleasant emotion caused by the belief that someone or something is dangerous, likely to cause pain, or a threat and be afraid of (someone or something) as likely to be dangerous, painful, or threatening."

Fear can cloud our minds, affect our judgment and cause us to make the wrong decision. I remember panicking during the market crash that I sold my stocks at the wrong time, costing me thousands of dollars in losses, only to see the stocks go back up. For me, fear is simply not trusting God.

We fear about not having money to pay our bills because we don't trust that God can provide; we fear for the safety of our children and loved ones because we don't trust that God owns them and will take care of them; we may fear getting fired because we don't trust God's ability through us. I can go on and on.

Fear has different faces such as worry, anxiety and stress. Fear hides under these types of labels and people don't even realize it. Worry, anxiety and stress have a root of fear but their corresponding result is the same. It paralyzes our ability to be productive, thus hindering us from accomplishing what we are supposed to do.

According to 2 Timothy 1:7, "*... God has not given us a spirit of fear, but of power and of love and of a sound mind.*" He did not give us a spirit of fear, which means that fear is given. When something is given, it must also be received. If I offer my friend Jan a red shirt, she has a choice whether to take it or not. The fullness of that offer will not materialize if the offer is not accepted. For that statement to come to fruition, the item must be received. I can either come home with the same red shirt in my possession, or Jan can go home with it. Therefore, we can only have fear if we accept it!

When I got that revelation, it changed the way I approached my life when fear knocked at my door. I love to travel and I've never had issues with being on a plane. I enjoy it, however, on a two-hour flight within the US, out of the blue, fear crept into my space. I felt anxious being on the plane – like I was losing air and couldn't breathe. The need to stand up and leave the plane began to overwhelm me. I knew then that I immediately had to rebuke those feelings, otherwise they would cripple me. I prayed, *Fear, according to 2 Timothy 1:17, I have not been given a spirit of fear but of power, love and a sound mind. Therefore, I am not receiving you, spirit of fear. Fear is given, and I am not accepting you in my life. So in the Name of Jesus, get out!* It immediately left!

We have a choice to allow the spirit of fear in and be crippled by it, or shut the door of our soul to it. We must do it immediately and nip it in the bud, because once it is in, it is harder to get out.

If you are suffering from fear, one of the first questions is, "When did you receive the red shirt?" (I am just using the red shirt as an analogy.) The question is,

When did it start?

When did you first have a fear of flying, of spiders, or of losing your parents?

It is important to know when it began, because the first time you experienced a particular type of fear is what we call the entry point that the enemy used as an open door to begin harassing you.

Someone can develop a fear of abandonment during a divorce, or when a parent goes home to be with the Lord. The enemy can come in and start giving thoughts of abandonment and fear of the consequence of being abandoned, like not having financial security, protection, and loneliness. That is all it takes. Next thing you know, the same person might find themselves controlling a relationship for fear of being abandoned again.

Fear can be crippling. I remember driving through the winding road of the mountains of West Ohio, driving flawlessly at about 70 miles an hour, when the thought came to me to look at the right side of the road to see how high I was. I now became conscious of the winding road and the height, fearful that if I swerved, I would fall off the cliff. The thought came out of nowhere!

I have already given some insights into the power of our minds and thoughts, so I hope we can see it here. Suddenly, I found myself slowing down and becoming more cautious in my driving on that winding road as I fought the fear of falling off the cliff. I had to overcome this fear to continue driving. Had I surrendered to the spirit of fear, I would not have been able to drive through the mountains again.

Fear is not a respecter of persons. It doesn't matter whether you are rich or poor, male or female, young or old, successful or not; this spirit will attack anyone who will accept it. One of the consequences of accepting it is its ability to paralyze us and stop us from accomplishing our tasks. It is undoubtedly the enemy of creativity. It comes in different ways, and it is good to know what it is so we can nip it in the bud immediately.

Fear of failure

Samuel Beckett, a Nobel Prize winner for Literature, was once asked, "What is the secret to being creative?"

He replied, "Fail, fail again, fail better!"

The fear of failure is one of the enemy's tactics to prevent us from inventing or releasing the Kingdom's creative ideas. It can creep in if fear convinces us that we don't have the skills to do it. It steals our confidence. We also see its effects every time we underestimate our ability, which causes us to preempt and justify our performance just in case we fail to perform. We see it when we worry that we will disappoint others. Some will go to the extent of not even trying at all!

It is not uncommon to hear stories of inventors and scientists who have invented world-changing products because they never allowed past failures to hinder their vision. Their vision and passion had overtaken them, so they couldn't afford to stop their journey even though the end of the tunnel was not in sight. Again, we have a choice; we can either allow fear to stop us at our first failure, or we can go on.

Thomas Edison had 1,000 unsuccessful attempts at inventing the light bulb. When a reporter asked, "How did it feel to fail 1,000 times?" Edison replied, "I didn't fail 1,000 times. The light bulb was an invention with 1,000 steps."

Have you ever imagined what our world would be like if Edison had stopped at the first "failure" – the first step?

I encourage you never to stop at the first step, but focus on the vision and the creative ideas God has given you to fulfill.

Fear of rejection

The fear of rejection is potent and can have a debilitating impact. Think of a time you were part of a group discussion. Some people always share while others don't even want to say a word. Sometimes people don't want to share because they fear their ideas will not be accepted. I used to be one of them! I used to be so quiet because I feared that whatever I said might not be good enough, or relevant to the discussion, until the Lord healed me of the fear of rejection.

Fear of making mistakes

I find that most people who are perfectionists also suffer from the fear of rejection, because in their attempt to be perfect, they end up being afraid to make mistakes. But others are so afraid to make mistakes that they don't do anything. George Bernard Shaw once said, "A life spent making mistakes is not only more honorable, but more useful than a life spent doing nothing." Some mistakes have actually led to accidental discoveries or inventions. An example was the Pacemaker.

> Dr. Wilson Greatbatch is responsible for this life-saving accidental scientific discovery made by mistake. It was in 1956 when he tried to make heart rhythm recorded, and while mixing up with some electronic component, he realized that

he actually made a device that helped unhealthy heart beat normally by sending shocks which stimulate heart muscles to pump blood properly.[6]

Similarly, some of my artwork turned out the way it did because I made a mistake, but as a result, the piece of art was better. According to Robert Anthony, "The more successful you are, the more mistakes you will make. People who don't do anything don't make mistakes."

These examples can increase our awareness of the enemy's tactic of using fear to stop the flow of our creativity and take us out of living in the creative realm. I encourage you to keep an open mind. Be bold. Don't be afraid to take risks, and don't allow the fear of mistakes to prevent you from creating or inventing. And most important, I pray you will no longer accept fear.

> *Lord, first of all, I repent for allowing fear to invade me and for accepting satan's schemes to deceive me by making me think my situation is bigger than You! I repent for all the fears, worries, and anxieties I have yielded to in my life because I didn't trust You. Lord, surround me with Your peace that surpasses all understanding. Guide my thoughts and calm the emotions that I am experiencing because of fear. Give me a vision of my future and hope for what is to come. I choose to trust You. I surrender my fears, worries, and anxieties to You and acknowledge that You are the One that covers me. You are my protection and security, and You will never forsake me, in the mighty Name of Jesus!*

PRAYER OF RELEASE #9 – FEAR NOT

Supernatural Decrees for Breakthrough

The Word says in Job 22:28, "decree a thing and it shall be established," therefore,

- I decree and declare that fear will never be my portion. Fear is given and can only derail me if I accept it. I choose not to receive or accept fear in my life. The fear of failure, rejection, or any other type of fear is not welcome in my house and my life! I will achieve my destiny.

- I decree and declare I disallow the spirit of fear to attack me. I will not be paralyzed by accepting it. I refuse to allow fear to stop the flow of my creativity and take me out of living in the creative realm.

- I decree and declare that I am not afraid of making mistakes because I learn from them. Peace is my guide and umpire. It shields and protects me from the enemy's arrows of fear.

- I decree and declare that I have supernatural faith to accomplish what God has purposed for me to achieve. I have the faith to move mountains and any obstacles the enemy has laid before me.

- I decree and declare that my past failures do not hinder my vision. My vision and passion compel me to continue my journey even when the end of the tunnel is not in sight.

LIFE APPLICATION SECTION

Memory Verse

For God has not given us a spirit of fear, but of power and of love and of a sound mind. *(2 Timothy 1:7)*

Reflections

1. What is fear?

   _____
   _____
   _____
   _____
   _____

2. Don't own fear. It doesn't originate with you. It is the opposite of faith and originates with satan as a demonic spirit. You can be free of that spirit because God did not give it to you. Write down the fears satan has inflicted on you and be specific. Once you have written them, declare 2 Timothy 1:17 over each one and repent for yielding to them. After you've repented, ask the Lord to heal you from these fears.

   _____
   _____
   _____
   _____
   _____

CHAPTER 10

HOW ARE YOU SPENDING YOUR TIME?

> ...whereas you do not know what will happen tomorrow. For what is your life? It is even a vapor that appears for a little time and then vanishes away.
> *(James 4:14)*

> Find time to create, even if it is only for 30-minutes.
> *(Carmela Myles)*

> Time is the most valuable thing a man can spend.
> *(Theophrastus)*

In this chapter, I aim to help you carve time out of your busy schedule to create and harness your creativity. I hope you will not fall into the category of always saying, I'm too busy, I don't have the time!

I woke up one day with a thought, *Busyness is created!* We have a choice to stay busy and fill our days with anything we want. Every day we are presented with many things to do. We have a choice to either do them or say no to them. I can say this much; if we know our purpose and assignment, we can easily say, No. The question is,

Why don't we have the time?

I pray that by the time we get to the end of this chapter, we will find the time to create!

To live in the creative realm, we must master the use of our time. One of the common denominators that we all have is time. Many people don't realize that time is a currency. This is why the verb *spend* is often used when it comes to time. We often ask questions like, Where did you spend your time? Who did you spend your time with? Or we say, I spent time with God today.

Time is a currency; we are always spending it. The question is,

How and where do we spend our time?

We are all given the same number of seconds and minutes a day. but not all of our outcomes are the same. Why? It depends on how we utilize our time. Every day twins are born that grow up in the same household with the same influences, yet they don't end up the same way. The difference is based on their decision of how they spend their time. Some use their time wisely; others end up wasting it. According to the *Merriam-Webster Dictionary*, *time* "is a measured or measurable period during which an action, process, or condition exists or continues." Ecclesiastes 3:1-2 states, *"There is a time for everything, and a season for every activity under the heavens: a time to be born and a time to die, a time to plant and a time to uproot."* This Scripture indicates that life is measured by time, so time wasted is life wasted!

I genuinely believe that each of us carries at least one creative idea that God wants to use to shape our world. That is why we must make time for creativity to flow through us, but we need to spend the time to create.

One of the nemeses of productive time is procrastination. Nike has it figured out: if you find yourself in a place of stagnation or procrastination, *Just do it!*

How are you Spending your Time?

Procrastination is the process of purposely delaying important things we need to do. Although this word is not in the Scripture, we can find words that best explain this habit: it is simply laziness!

> Laziness casts one into a deep sleep,
> And an idle person will suffer hunger.
> *(Proverbs 19:15)*

> Because of laziness the building decays,
> And through idleness of hands, the house leaks.
> *(Ecclesiastes 10:18)*

Even before the fall of man, God always intended for us to work. In the book of beginnings, Genesis 2:15 states, *"Then the Lord God took the man and put him in the garden of Eden to tend and keep it."* In this passage we find God put the man in the garden to tend and keep it. Some translations state: to cultivate, dress, and work. The Hebrew word states that work is an act of worship.

Our work is our worship! We are missing the act of worshipping our God who created us if we don't work. Laziness is not worship. It is dishonoring to God. While growing up, I always heard my elders saying, *"If you don't work, you don't eat."* According to Ecclesiastes 10:18, *"Because of laziness the building decays, And through idleness of hands, the house leaks."* That sounds like procrastination to me.

I remember a rental house that we entrusted to some people. Our house manager delayed, or procrastinated in fixing a leak in the bathroom, and the leak damaged the entire wall of the bathroom and the dining room on the other side of it. A $200-dollar repair ended up costing thousands. We would have saved thousands of dollars had it been fixed immediately. Can you identify with that?

I remember a friend who had a toothache. We kept telling him to go to the dentist, but our friend continued to procrastinate, resulting in his tooth having to be pulled. He could have saved his tooth had he gone to the dentist earlier. Now he needs braces because his teeth shifted to fill the space where the pulled tooth had been.

Procrastination certainly sabotages one's creativity. It is like a block in a drainage pipe that stops the water from flowing. Procrastination blocks the creative flow of the Holy Spirit causing products assigned to us not to be produced. My goal in this chapter is to activate your creativity so you can create by encouraging you to use your time wisely through proper time management.

In this age of technology, we have so many distractions – the internet, social media, TV, Netflix, and digital games. Many believers are caught up wasting their time surfing the internet and playing games. I remember having lunch with friends. One of them couldn't focus on our amazing conversation because her eyes were glued to her phone while she was playing games. Zig Ziglar's famous quote: "I am always present."

We need to be more intentional in being present when we are with friends, family, and those with whom we are interacting. Even children are caught up in this digital world. I have seen parents too busy to take care of them, so they give them an iPad, or phone to play games, even while eating at a restaurant. What happened to the tradition of parents and children sitting together during dinner and using that precious time to talk about how their day went? Some of our children are not being properly trained and raised to pray and think creatively because those who are supposed to be training them are too distracted. That is why we must be intentional and deliberate in appropriating one of our precious commodities – time.

Activate creativity through proper time management

1. **Goal setting** - *Merriam-Webster Dictionary* defines a *goal* as the end toward which effort is directed; According to *MindTools.com*, it is a process that starts with careful consideration of what you want to achieve, and ends with a lot of hard work to actually do it. In between, there are some very well-defined steps that

transcend the specifics of each goal. Knowing these steps will allow you to formulate goals that you can accomplish.

What does the Bible say about it? According to Luke 14:28, *"For which of you, intending to build a tower, does not sit down first and count the cost, whether he has enough to finish it…."*

Proverbs 15:8 states, *"The plans of the diligent lead to profit as surely as haste leads to poverty."*

We are advised to plan. Luke got it! His statement implies we need a set goal before we can build something, or start a project. I'm sure that we can all relate to this. How often have we done something out of impulse, and through haste, lost our hard-earned money and wasted our precious time?

Goal setting is one of the primary recommendations of time management motivators. Successful people have short-term and long-term goals. It allows them to properly focus and concentrate on their day-to-day tasks so they can efficiently use their time to reach the goal they put upon themselves.

Do you have a long-term goal?
What about a short-term goal?

If you don't, I encourage you to get a notebook and start writing your goals. Something happens when you put your goals on paper. Let us learn from Habakkuk: *"Write the vision, And make it plain on tablets, That he may run who reads it"* (Habakkuk 2:2).

The more you read the goals you've written, the more you ensure that they become embedded into your subconscious mind. Your subconscious mind sees them as a reality and eventually agrees with what you have on paper.

2. **Use a time planner**

   A time planner lets you see the big picture of what you are trying to accomplish so you can effectively plan your days, weeks, months, and years accordingly. It allows you to schedule your meetings, tasks, events, and appointments to prevent running out of time or forgetting essential tasks that must be done.

3. **Put together a "to-do list."**

   I am convinced that one of the enemy's strategies to get us to fail is forgetfulness and short-term memory loss. I have missed so many appointments, meetings, and important matters I had to deal with simply because I forgot! I have found out most of my tasks are accomplished more efficiently when I have a *"to-do list."* It has been proven that there is a 25 percent increase in efficiency the first day we start using a list. Below are some of the benefits of having one:

   1. *It creates order* – A "to-do list" puts our life in order and gives us a big picture of what tasks we need to accomplish during the day. It gives us a good feeling of knowing what is ahead so we can strategize and prioritize the tasks at hand. It makes us remember things to ensure nothing falls through the cracks of our busy lives.

   2. *It creates accountability* – Writing down tasks we need to accomplish gives us a sense of accountability. When we write, we become more conscious of what needs to be done, making us accountable to perform and finish it. Missing deadlines becomes a myth in our life.

   3. *It boosts productivity* – It gives us more focus to concentrate on our list, thus avoiding any distractions presented before us. If we get distracted, we can always go back where we left

off without thinking about what's next. It is a no-brainer; our productivity can only increase!

These are just some of the benefits of keeping a "to-do list." The pitfalls of not having one are disorganization, disorder, and a failure to create what we've been assigned. I encourage you to develop the habit of writing down a "to-do list." If you are already doing it, I praise God for your diligence! You are a productive person.

4. *Learn how to delegate* – Part of efficient time management is knowing how to delegate. Some of us are used to doing things ourselves – an effort that may be wasting our precious time.

Two are always better than one. Even Jesus sent His disciples two by two. What if we were three, four, or five? We could accomplish more if more people were helping us. Therefore, since time is an expensive currency, it is best to hire out tasks others can do, or delegate to someone else some of your own day-to-day tasks like cooking, mowing the lawn, or filing receipts, and thereby utilize your time better.

I praise God for our assistants and destiny helpers! When we moved to Tennessee, a dear friend and ministry partner helped us organize our products in our garage. She and her friends spent at least a week working on it while we were ministering outside the country. My husband and I saved much time that we used instead to continue traveling and speaking to God's people.

4. **Prioritize your tasks**

Have you ever gone to bed at night with thoughts and determination to accomplish specific tasks the following day, but have woken up to unanticipated hurdles, one after another? I have many of those days.

Prioritizing is essential because it disciplines us to perform each task based on its urgency and importance. Stephen Covey said, "The key is not to prioritize what's on your schedule, but to schedule your priorities." Below are tools we can implement to help us prioritize our life.

The Eisenhower Matrix Prioritization Rule

This is a tool that helps people improve their effectiveness. President Dwight Eisenhower developed the concept behind what would later be called the Eisenhower Matrix. He used it to help him prioritize and deal with the many high-stakes issues he faced as a USA Army general, then as Supreme Allied Commander of NATO Forces, and eventually as president of the United States.[7]

This prioritization tool helps us segregate tasks based on their urgency and importance. It allows us to separate tasks based on important vs. unimportant, and urgent vs. not urgent.

As we learn to prioritize, we can certainly carve out time for creativity. I have included a graphic below for a better understanding of this tool. I find it very helpful. Once we have segregated our tasks, we should only be doing the top two quadrants ourselves, and be delegating, or deleting the bottom ones.

How are you Spending your Time?

The 80-20 Rule

The 80-20 rule, also known as the Pareto principle, is a known phenomenon in business and economics that gives us insight that 20 percent of effort, or input yields 80 percent of results or outputs. It helps companies and businesses organize and prioritize their resources to increase productivity and achieve a much more desirable bottom line.

There are so many applications of the 80-20 rule; Here are a few to help you understand this concept better:

- 80 percent of Italy's wealth belonged to only 20 percent of the population – This was Pareto's observation that led him to discover this principle.

- 20 percent of the input creates 80 percent of the results – This principle often proves that 80 percent of a company's revenue comes from 20 percent of its customers. Some companies have applied this principle by focusing on their customers, giving them more attention and more customer care, and by targeting marketing ideas to help them use their company's goods and services.

- 20 percent of workers produce 80 percent of results – When I was a new believer, my pastor would comment that I am "part of the 20 percent." The concept is that the church can perform its functions and activities with 20 percent of its volunteers and helpers.

Benefits of 80-20 Rule

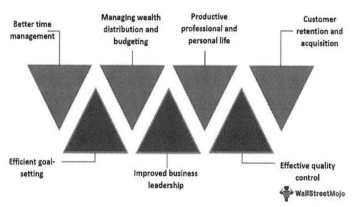

Free image from WallstreetMojo.com

How do we apply this rule to time management and activating our creativity? The 80-20 rule can be simplified in three key steps:

1. **Identify what our key results or goals are** – Since this book is about rekindling and rediscovering your creative nature. Identify what you believe God has given you to create or produce.

2. **Apply the 80/20 rule to prioritize our tasks** – determine the crucial tasks you need to perform to accomplish the majority of your creative ideas – those that you cannot delegate to anyone because you are the main person that can accomplish them, like significant decision-making, designing a new brand of bag, architectural design development. These are also tasks that you love and enjoy doing as a creative thinker – that you can do faster than other people around you who don't have the same passion for them.

   Once you have identified the main tasks that you can do, then delegate the rest to others. As the architect, you can delegate the drafting, printing, construction documents, and bidding of the project. As a bag designer, you can delegate the other tasks to a seamstress who can sew and cut the materials.

I am very creative, always thinking of products I can produce. On the other hand, I wouldn't say I like paperwork. My receipts are all over the place, and it takes me time to organize them. So I just hired someone who loves that kind of work. Now I can use my time for creativity.

Believe me, there's always someone out there who loves doing the task that's tough for you, but don't give them flyers or brochures to design if that's your talent. It'll be a nightmare for them! Are you getting it?

3. **Protect the most important activities from the least important ones** – This is when we apply priority management.
We are bombarded every day with major and minor tasks.
The key is to identify and separate the most critical activities from the least important ones so we can prioritize our schedules to be more productive with our day. Our priorities must align with our short-term goals, which must be tied to our long-term goals.
Concentrating on the least essential activities will be a disaster if we have insufficient time to meet our essential deadlines.

- Twenty percent of the activity is responsible for 80 percent of the result – I strongly believe in having a very close relationship with the Holy Spirit. If I apply the 80-20 rule to our private and prayer life, I can honestly say that if we spent at least 20 percent of our time with the Holy Spirit, we would attain 80 percent of our production and creativity goals because of those intimate moments with Him.
Most of Francis' and my most creative ideas and solutions have come after spending time with Him. I remember when the Lord told me to print my artwork on blankets – a product

that became one the best sellers for our ministry. Then He gave me the idea to print my artwork on fabric. I am now producing dresses and shirts with my fabric.

- When I was in Cameroon, I hired a seamstress to sew a dress. She told her friend that she was creating a dress from a prophetic print. The friend took some excess fabric, wrapped it in her hair, and prayed for the Lord to restore her inner beauty. The friend also suffered from bloating, so she had been very limited in the dresses she could wear. But when she woke up, her stomach had a pronounced change. The bloating had gone down!

Many other time management tools could help us manage our time to be more creative. Find the one that works for you.

Redeeming your time

The good thing is, there is always good news! The Bible has given us hope that we can redeem our time. Here are some Scriptures that give us this hope:

> Redeeming the time, because the days are evil.
> *(Ephesians 5:16)*

> Walk in wisdom toward those who are *outside, redeeming the time.*
> *(Colossians 4:5)*

> So teach us to number our days, That we may gain a heart of wisdom.
> *(Psalms 90:12)*

The word redeeming in two of these verses is from the Greek word, *exagorazó*, which means to buy up, i.e., ransom, or figuratively means to rescue from loss. Therefore, it is not too late to redeem our time by starting to take ownership and control of it to maximize and effectively use it for the Kingdom. We must intentionally put purpose in everything we do, and it is imperative that we redeem our time by using it to increase our value, activate our creativity, and build His Kingdom. We need to be ready in and out of season.

Let me pray for you now:

> *I decree and declare you walk in grace to be a good steward of your time. I pray that you will not waste the time God have given you but instead that you use your time wisely to accomplish every task He has assigned you to do. I declare that your time will produce quality fruit for people to feed on. It will be used to create the canvas that God wants you to paint for His glory. May the Lord redeem your time to seize every opportunity He has presented. May God maximize it by increasing your value and activating your creativity. May you never spend time again getting drunk from all the distractions the world is offering but use your time to effectively plan and seek the Lord's face so that the kingdoms of this world become His Kingdom in the Mighty Name of Jesus!*

PRAYER OF RELEASE #10
– HOW ARE YOU SPENDING YOUR TIME?

Supernatural Decrees for Breakthrough

The Word says in Job 22:28, "decree a thing and it shall be established," therefore,

- I decree and declare that my time is redeemed. I am efficient in the use of my time. I have wisdom to carve out time to plant my creative seeds.

- I decree and declare that I disallow the spirit of procrastination to sabotage my creativity. Procrastination is no longer my portion and it can no longer delay the manifestation of my creative ideas.

- I decree and declare that I use my time wisely. I have the grace to set my goals, create my schedule, plan my life, prioritize my tasks, and delegate the tasks that consume my time.

- I decree and declare that my creative ideas will not be stolen through laziness. My productivity is increased because the spirit of laziness no longer operates in me.

- I decree and declare that I will not die before my appointed time. I will accomplish all that God has given me. The spirit of delay will no longer create havoc in my life to prevent me from accessing my full potential.

LIFE APPLICATION SECTION

Memory Verse

There is a time for everything, and a season for every activity under the heavens: a time to be born and a time to die, a time to plant and a time to uproot. *(Ecclesiastes 3:1-2)*

Reflections

1. Write down some ways to carve out your time to activate your creativity.

   _____
   _____
   _____
   _____
   _____

2. As an exercise, write down your current *"to-do list"* and apply one of the tools discussed to prioritize the tasks.

   _____
   _____
   _____
   _____
   _____

CHAPTER 11

HOW TO ACTIVATE YOUR CREATIVITY

> Do you see a man skillful and experienced in his work? He will stand [in honor] before kings; He will not stand before obscure men.
>
> *(Proverbs 22:29)*

> Creativity can be learned as learning to read.
>
> *(Ken Robinson)*

> Jews believe that people are creators, not consumers. The role of humans is to improve and perfect God's creations through work, creation, and innovation.
>
> *(H.W. Charles)*

I have already shown you that creativity can be activated, because it has been given to us by God. We just have to discover what He has deposited in us. But creativity can also be learned. It is up to us to carve out time and create an environment that can enhance our creativity. I cannot stress enough the importance of honing our skills and becoming an expert in our field. Our work must always glorify God. We have to make sure we make God look good! After all, He is the Master Craftsman, isn't He?

How to Activate your Creativity

The Spirit of Excellence must be upon us to produce first-class products that can become legendary – useful and enjoyed for years to come. Our work should never fall into a stage of mediocrity, or into the abyss of obscurity.

The wisdom of Proverbs 22:29 states that those who are skillful and experienced will stand before kings and not stand before obscure men. Obscure men are described as those who are low in rank and unknown. Our goal should be to influence kings and those who are born influencers so that the kingdom of this world can become the Kingdom of our God. Our creativity can take us to these spheres of influence.

I can humbly say that some of my products are now in the hands of government officials and kings in the marketplace because I have continuously honed my abilities to produce better digital arts. My work through the years has improved because I purposed in my heart to continue to grow in my skills. I have been surprised lately with some testimonies of healing emerging when some have used my prophetic scarves and blankets. I believe healings are happening because of my desire for the Lord to release the unseen into the seen. In my opinion, as a result I have produced products that the Holy Spirit has influenced, or anointed, to advance the Kingdom of God through the arts.

Discover and activate your creativity

Pablo Picasso once said, "Every child is an artist, the problem is staying an artist when you grow up."

I now want to give you some tools to start activating your creativity.

People are always asking me how I produce my art. I am sure that there are many ways for one's creativity to be activated, but below are my life-learned methods I employ to remain creative:

1. **Set aside time for creativity** – I have given you some tools and ways to manage your time so you can free up time to allow for creativity. We must always carve out time in our busy schedules

for this purpose. It is the only way we can create or produce something without our busy lives taking over. We must find time to incorporate it into our goal setting and to-do list and schedule it on our calendar.

It takes 21 days to create a habit. Creating goals and schedules forces us to create habits supporting creativity. Make these simple tasks a priority, and watch your creative flow increase! It will be amazing to see what happens when time spent on social media and surfing the net is replaced by time for creativity.

I must admit that writing this book – my first one – was not easy. I had to force myself to write, and sometimes I would reread it and couldn't believe what I had written. I've never liked to write; it was not my favorite part of creating, but the Lord has clearly given me the grace to tap into my dormant potential to write. It is a talent I have discovered that I am capable of doing, but certainly not without sacrificing time for doing things I would prefer to do.

2. **Exercise** – It is never too late to exercise. Why we need to exercise is a no-brainer. The benefits of exercising include increased stamina, improved health, better focus, and clarity in thinking. Regular physical exercise helps to deliver oxygen and nutrients to vital parts of our body. It is known to relieve stress, depression, fear, and anxiety.

If we are physically fit and able, we can do more and think better, thus increasing our productivity and creativity. An article called *Regular Exercise can boost Creativity* by Huffpost.com states that "Specifically, researchers noted that regular exercise seems to be associated with improved divergent and convergent thinking, which are considered the two components of creative thinking; the former involves thinking of multiple solutions for one problem, while the latter involves thinking of one solution for a problem." The same article mentioned an experiment

"…to determine the association between exercise and creativity, researchers had 48 athletes (who exercised at least four times a week) and 48 non-athletes (who didn't regularly exercise) do a creativity test. For the first part of the test, the participants had to think of alternate uses for a pen and write them down. Then, the participants were presented with a series of three words and asked to find the link that connected them (for instance, 'long' connects the words 'time,' 'hair,' and 'stretch'). Researchers found that the regular exercisers did better on the second task compared with those who didn't regularly exercise.[8]

According to Lorenza Colzato, a cognitive psychologist at Leiden University in the Netherlands, "Exercising on a regular basis may thus act as a cognitive enhancer promoting creativity in inexpensive and healthy ways."

I concur with this statement because I experience mental alertness and a creative flow every time I exercise.

I encourage you to read, or watch the YouTube video of Wang Deshun. He is an 80-year-old Chinese runway model with a fitness regime. He believes that old age should never be used as an excuse for giving up.[9] He started exercising when he was in his fifties. He looks young and muscular, and it is for an excellent reason.

As you can see, it is never too late to jump on the bandwagon. I encourage you to start exercising if you haven't yet included it in your daily routine, even if it only begins with five minutes. The benefit is going to be substantial.

You want to make sure you accomplish God's assignment in your life, since there are men and women of God who died early because they did not take care of their physical temple. I certainly don't want to be part of that statistic!

3. **Eat healthily** – Like exercising, we think better when we eat better. I have often experienced sleepiness after eating certain foods, especially comfort and junk foods! In these times, I have stopped working because my creative flow was hindered by what I put in my mouth.

   A friend of ours was diagnosed with high blood pressure. Her doctor warned her to stop eating fried food, but she never heeded his advice and continued to eat it because it was her favorite. One day she was rushed to the hospital, but they could not save her life.

   We eat to live, but we don't live to eat. We become what we eat, and are what we eat!

   We don't realize how much our lives are influenced by food until it isn't there. Have you tried fasting? It is always during a fast that I realize how much of my life is centered on eating.

4. **Take a creative stroll** – Stanford researchers found that walking, as opposed to sitting, improves creativity. Mark Zuckerberg of Facebook and the late Steve Jobs of Apple are both known for walking while conducting their meetings. Marilyn Oppezzo, a Standford doctoral graduate in educational psychology, and Daniel Schwartz, a Stanford Graduate School of Education professor, found that walking either indoors or outdoors similarly boosted creative inspiration. Across the board, creativity levels were consistently and significantly higher for those who walked instead of just sat.

   In addition, "...a study published in the International *Journal of Stroke* showed that those who became fit later in life cut their risk of a potentially deadly stroke in half. It's not a stretch to say that just a little walking (or other aerobic activity) grows your brain. Researchers have found that regular aerobic exercise appears to increase the size of the hippocampus, the region of the brain responsible for memory. And the benefits can be pretty

How to Activate your Creativity

immediate. A University of Maryland study of people ages 55 to 85, for instance, showed that a single session of exercise increased activation in the brain circuits associated with memory."[10]

Some of my creative ideas come when I walk outside while admiring the beauty of God's creation, or while I'm walking on our treadmill. The benefit of walking to have a healthy mind can therefore help harness our creativity.

5. **Put yourself in a creative environment** – We can be creative anywhere, but some need the right environment to be more creative. Some people can write while the TV is on and the music is blasting. Others need a quiet environment with softer music to function creatively. Francis falls in the first category, and I fall in the second. Can you imagine what it's like when we both work together creatively? He has learned to put on a headset to help me work, or at times he will go out of the house to write, and vice versa. I do the same thing to create my digital arts. So between my husband and I, we have managed to establish a creative environment for our creative juices to flow.

Some companies purposely foster a very pleasing workplace to create a culture of promoting creativity. We find that such companies have a higher rate of happy and productive employees. Google provides staff perks like free food and gym membership. They also have bowling alleys and pool tables. They are one of the first to offer this type of incentive to harness the creativity of their staff. Others have followed suit. Companies are always offering courses to enhance people's skills.

When I used to work for Pricewaterhouse Coopers in Manhattan, the company sent us to Stone Mountain, Georgia, for one of our training sessions. During our break, my colleagues and I went walking and hiking to the top of Stone Mountain. We had so much fun! We were never bored while we attended their training.

6. **Ask questions** – Don't ever be afraid to ask questions. There is never a stupid question. I always say that because I'm always asking questions; that is just my personality. I'm able to navigate life better if I ask questions. As an experienced questioner (Francis actually calls me that), I learn more, and some of my questions have led to answers that have helped me improve my skills, or any project I'm working on at the time.

7. **Don't be afraid to brainstorm** – According to *Merriam-Webster Dictionary*, *brainstorming* is a group problem-solving technique that involves the spontaneous contribution of ideas from all members of the group:

    …brainstorming can generate some wonderful ideas. Some of the most challenging problems in the ministry have been resolved through this process. In addition, some of the most successful strategies, projects, and ideas our ministry is still experiencing have resulted from brainstorming with our leaders. One of our rules is that there is never a dumb idea. What amazes me with brainstorming is when one creative idea starts building on another. The result is very fulfilling; it's like puzzle pieces coming together to reveal the big picture. We all knew the project would not have been finalized if the other person's idea had not been brought to the table.

8. **Join a group club and take classes** – We are in the world of social groups, clubs, and associations for special interests and passion. There is a group for every interest, from photography, to car enthusiasts, to sports. You can join groups to meet and learn from people with the same passion. I have learned many Photoshop tricks just by watching some online classes.

9. **Practice** – "Practice makes perfect," is a famous saying. Isn't that true? Specific commands in Photoshop, one of the digital

software programs I use to create my arts, are second nature to me because I have used them so many times. I don't even think about it. It's like riding a bike. Once you learn and continuously ride it, you just go without thinking! I cannot stress this enough.

I believe that excellence is also attained through practice and repetition. I don't think most of the gold medalists received their gold by practicing once a month. That's impossible! Their parents will be the first to tell us how they painfully sacrificed times with friends and family and missed birthdays and important family functions because their son or daughter had to practice. Again, it is a matter of choice.

10. **Find a mentor** – Mentorship is probably one of the critical relationships people miss. A mentor is someone who is very integral in our life. I am who I am today because I surrounded myself with mentors who helped me hone my skills. According to *Mindtools.com*:

> A mentorship is a relationship between two people where the individual with more experience, knowledge, and connections is able to pass along what they have learned to a more junior individual within a certain field. The more senior individual is the mentor, and the more junior individual is the mentee.

100 Black Men of America is an organization that offers mentorship. According to its website, it is recognized as the nation's top African American-led mentoring organization. They say that all youth are born with privilege, opportunities, or a positive network, yet some are raised throughout their lives thinking they'll never be able to live the life they want. That is because of their environment and the people who surround them daily. While every person should be able to create the life they've always wanted, The 100 Black Men of America organization is

dedicated to providing that opportunity to the African American community.

Do you have a mentor? I encourage you to pray and ask the Lord to bring you the right mentors. In the meantime, many online teachings can help you in your journey. I have been blessed with relationships with gifted mentors, but I cannot deny the teachings and wisdom I have gained by listening online to men and women I will never meet. Even so, I have still gained mentorship through their teachings.

I know of an artist whose skills in painting improved to the point that she can now command a higher price for her work because an artist mentored her through an E-course.

11. **Find time to be alone in solitude** – We live in an era of too much information. We are constantly bombarded with information from social media, news, and the web. In addition, we have too many apps available for playing games and listening to podcasts and videos. Our time is consumed with digesting too much information, which takes us away from organic thinking – times when we quiet ourselves and detox from information overload.

How can we possibly hear the voice of God if the noise of this world constantly surrounds us?

Find time to quiet yourself and meditate!

12. **Strengthen our spiritual muscles** – We cannot be deceived to think that our creativity can be activated without strengthening our spiritual life. Part of living in the creative realm and activating our creativity is to make it a priority to strengthen our walk with the Lord. Therefore, I have included some of the ways we can do it as follows:

How to Activate your Creativity

1. *Read the Word* – We cannot afford *not* to read the Word. It says in Mark 13:22, *"For false christ and false prophets will rise and show signs and wonders to deceive, if possible, even the elect."* We should undoubtedly include reading the Bible as part of our daily routine, otherwise the enemy can deceive and derail us off the path the Lord has set before us.
We cannot possibly survive eating yesterday's manna. Every day we must eat fresh Bread; we must read the Word. Even in the natural, we can't eat stale bread! Just as our bodies need fresh food, our spirits also need fresh food.

2. *Pray* – 1 Thessalonians 5:17, *"…pray without ceasing."* Prayer is integral in our walk with God. Paul advised us to pray without ceasing. Without ceasing means to pray continuously, nonstop. That means we are encouraged to pray in all our circumstances for healing, deliverance, wisdom, and when we need to make a decision. It is a powerful way to cause things in the spirit to manifest on earth. Pray and call forth your creative ideas into manifestation. Call forth what is not as though it was through prayer.

3. *Fast* – Fasting is a time to humble ourselves and seek God's face so we can hear Him. There are many reasons why people fast, but we can fast for clarity concerning the creative seeds He has given us, to hear clear instructions and get wisdom on how to proceed to get it done.

4. *Spend time with God* – I can't emphasize enough the importance of spending time with God. Most of my creative ideas came explicitly while spending time with the Lord. I have also elaborated on this in Chapter 3: Communion with the Holy Spirit.

5. *Speak in tongues* – Many people don't realize what happens when we speak in tongues. It builds our spirit spiritually and morally through God. I love to pray in tongues because it releases me from thinking. I find it easier and more effective. Even though I don't know what I am praying about, I know in my heart that I am accomplishing a lot in the spirit. I remember when the unction to pray in tongues came upon me while babysitting my pastor's son Jon. He could also pray in the Spirit. I told him to pray in tongues, and about ten minutes after we prayed, he took his skateboard and hit a tree. We both knew Jon could have been badly injured if we had not prayed in tongues. Only God knows what would have happened if we had not obeyed the unction of the Lord to pray.

6. *Rest and have fun!* – God is not a taskmaster. We can't forget to rest and have fun. I know some people who can't have fun because they are always working. They don't have time to spend with their family. They come home exhausted and fall asleep just to wake up in the morning and do it again. Like a car, we cannot move without oil. We cannot run down our bodies to a point where we are no longer productive because we run out of energy. Even God rested on the seventh day as He admired what He's created and said, "It is good!" We need to take time to rest and see what we have already accomplished.

Increase your value

Now that I have shared some of the ways we can activate our creativity. I want to encourage everyone to start increasing their value through their creativity as an artist or creative person in your field of expertise. Myles Munroe used to say, "If you want to become successful, seek to become a person of value. <u>Your value in life is determined by the problems you solve through your gift.</u>" People will not seek us if we cannot solve their problems. Our gifts should make room for us.

I will end with this story:

> A father said to his daughter, "You have graduated with honors. Here is a jeep I bought many years ago. It is pretty old now. But before I give it to you, take it to the used car lot downtown and tell them I want to sell it and see how much they offer you for it." The daughter went to the used car lot, returned to her father, and said, "They offered me $1,000 because they said it is pretty worn out."
>
> The father said now, "Take it to the pawn shop." The daughter went to the pawn shop, returned to her father, and said, "The pawn shop offered only $100 because it is an old jeep."
>
> The father asked his daughter to go to a Jeep club and show them the Jeep. The daughter then took the Jeep to the club, returned, and told her father, "Some people in the club offered $100,000 for it because "it's an iconic Jeep and sought by many collectors."
>
> The father said to his daughter, "The right place values you the right way." If you are not valued, do not be angry, it means you are in the wrong place. Those who know your value are those who appreciate you....Never stay in a place where no one sees your value."

If we know our worth, we will not underestimate or undervalue our creativity. We will never be discouraged if others don't see and appreciate it.

LIVING IN THE CREATIVE REALM

When I started to sell prints of my artwork, I thought of selling them for $30 per 16x20 size print. Then I heard in my spirit, "Is that all your worth? The time you spent to create it and the time you spent in prayer to seek Me and have My Mind, you think that's all your worth?" That's all it took! I changed the price to $60 per print and have been selling them for that price since then. I'm amazed how many people are buying them for that price.

Our value is also determined by how we see ourselves. As the famous saying goes "You are what you think you are!" Isn't that true? Now the question is,

How valuable are you?

Let me pray for you.

> *Lord in the Mighty name of Jesus. I decree and declare the Spirit of Creativity flows through you. May God activate you and take you to another level of freedom to create. May He change how you see yourself and give you the grace to continue increasing your value and worth. May God heal you from any blockages that make you think otherwise. May He make you a vessel of excellence to show off His masterpiece of creativity through your hands. May He release the wisdom to create. The world needs the products and creative ideas He has deposited in you, so let it manifest, now in Jesus' Name!*

Prayer of Release #11 – How to Activate Your Creativity

Supernatural Decrees for Breakthrough

The Word says in Job 22:28, "decree a thing and it shall be established," therefore,

- I decree and declare that the Spirit of Excellence is upon me to produce first-class products that become legendary for years to come. My work will never be mediocre or disappear into obscurity.

- I decree and declare I have the grace to increase my value. I invest in activating my creativity and the skills that God has given me, and in learning my trade.

- I decree and declare that I will not be taken before my appointed time. I choose to eat heathy, exercise regularly, and pray without ceasing to access God's creative seeds that He has deposited in me.

- I decree and declare that I discover everything God has given me to create heaven's projects and products for the advancement of the Kingdom. I do not hoard my gifts, but continue to produce until every task assigned to me is accomplished.

- I decree and declare that I know my worth; I do not underestimate or undervalue my gift of creativity, and I am never discouraged if people don't see and appreciate it because I know my worth.

- I decree and declare that I follow and obey all commandments God has commanded me today. I am careful to observe them that I may live and multiply and go in and possess the land that the Lord swore to give to my forefathers.

LIFE APPLICATION SECTION

Memory Verse

Do you see a man skillful and experienced in his work? He will stand [in honor] before kings; He will not stand before obscure men. *(Proverbs 22:29)*

Reflections

1. What are some ways you have already begun to activate your creativity? Based on what you have learned from this chapter, what will you start implementing to discover more of your creativity?

   _____
   _____
   _____
   _____

2. What is the Spirit of Excellence, and why do you think it is essential to have it in your life?

   _____
   _____
   _____
   _____

CHAPTER 12

THE POWER TO CREATE WEALTH THROUGH CREATIVITY

> And you shall remember the Lord your God, for it is He who gives you power to get wealth, that He may establish His covenant which He swore to your fathers, as it is this day.
>
> *(Deuteronomy 8:18)*

> If money is your hope for independence, you will never have it. The only real security that a man will have in this world is a reserve of knowledge, experience, and ability.
>
> *(Henry Ford)*

The Lord emphasized to the Israelites how important it was to remember His commandments, as we see in Deuteronomy 8:1-2:

Every commandment which I command you today you must be careful to observe, that you may live and multiply, and go in and possess the land of which the Lord swore to your fathers. And you shall remember that the Lord your God led you all the way these forty years in the wilderness, to humble you and test you, to know what was in your heart, whether you would keep His commandments or not.

God is saying the same to us today. We must be careful to observe these commandments because He wants us to experience and have the following:

1. **Life** - Obedience to every commandment He has commanded us ensures us a long life to fulfill every assignment God has given us. The late Dr. Myles Munroe always talked about dying empty, which means that by the time we go to be with the Lord, we are emptied of every assignment He has bestowed upon our lives for the advancement of His Kingdom. Dr. Munroe called the graveyard the richest place on earth because of all the God-given poetry, books, movies, witty inventions, technologies, and assignments buried there, never to be manifested on earth. Those whom God had assigned and instructed to fulfill these assignments did not properly steward their lives to ensure their manifestation while they were alive. The assignments died with them!

   This revelation forever changed me.

   Living longer allows God's creativity given us to be released. The books, movies, divine inventions, and technologies He has given us to steward must be properly appropriated during our lifetimes. The challenge to you, the reader is to discover all He has given you.

   > What are your projects?
   > Are they being done?
   > Have you even started working on them?

2. **Multiplication** – Obedience to every commandment He has given us also helps our ability to multiply.

   I truly believe God's multiplication differs from the worldly concept of multiplying. The world's egotistical nature results in multiplication for self-preservation instead of for God's purposes to be accomplished here on earth and preserved for generations to come. We need to multiply ourselves and our achievements. We need to impart our God-given wisdom to the next generation.

Future artists, authors, dancers, actors, inventors, scientists, doctors, engineers, and lawyers must convey the message and purpose of the Kingdom in everything they produce. It is a divine necessity. We cannot hoard what God has given us for our own preservation. These things must be taught and distributed.

The only way for the next generation to accomplish this task is by us becoming their mentors and imparting the talents and creativity God has given us.

I remember going to Zimbabwe to one of the biggest churches to conduct our School of the Order of Melchizedek. We invited former Order of Melchizedek students to be instructors in Zimbabwe. Francis and I could have done it ourselves, but Francis wanted to impart and mentor them so they could develop their gifts and then instruct others. We brought in at least seven instructors who were most appreciative. It is impossible to reach everyone.

We need to multiply! In that one situation, we multiplied ourselves by seven.

3. **Possession of the land that was promised to our forefathers** – Many of us do not have the concept of possessing land. That is why many believers still rent rather than own land. Land is connected to our destiny. It is part of our inheritance – God's covenant and dominion. This is very important. The first thing God promised Abraham was land, not people, as seen in Genesis 12:7, *"...then the LORD appeared to Abram and said, 'To your offspring I will give this land.' So he built an altar there to the LORD, who had appeared to him."* I believe that even the founding fathers of our great nation of America understood the importance of this point. According to the Fundamental Constitutions of North

The Power to Create Wealth Through Creativity

Carolina, 1669, *"No man shall be chosen a member of parliament who has less than five hundred acres of freehold within the precinct for which he is chosen; nor shall any have a vote in choosing the said member that hath less than fifty acres of freehold within the said precinct."* Talk about dominion through land ownership even in the voting system during that time![11]

I also want you to ponder the fact that land does not multiply. We cannot miss the opportunity to have land.

Why do many believers not possess land God has given them?

Lack of finances can be a reason. One of the ways we can acquire wealth can be through creativity so that owning land becomes a breeze.

Francis and I hold a substantial amount of land we have earmarked to be used as a city of refuge for orphans in Zambia. It was clearly a miracle to acquire this land, however we still need some finances to purchase it fully. One of our sources was the royalties we have received as a result of creativity released through the books and digital arts we have produced. We sell these products at conferences and thereby raise funds.

God's command

And yes, according to Deuteronomy 8:1, the Israelites were not just asked if they want to own land. They were commanded, that means they were instructed, ordered, charged, and sent. You might ask,

What does it have to do with living in the creative realm?

Being a landowner plays a significant role in activating the creative realm, plus more!

Our lives are based on the covenant and promises of God. We cannot access the full potential of our creativity if we are outside the boundaries of God's promises and His covenant. That is why it is essential to have an understanding and revelation of land ownership. In the particular passage above, you will find that remembering the Lord was required to achieve the following:

1. **Humble us** – Humility is accepting that creativity was never to come from our strength but through the power, grace, and mercy of the Living God. The Israelites wandered for 40 years and were stripped of everything they knew and possessed so God could show them He was God.

   To live in the creative realm, we must understand that we only have creativity because God gave it to us.

   My arts are created during times of divine inspiration and instructions. Sometimes, no matter what I do, I can't create because the inspiration of the Holy Spirit is not there. I learned to wait until I received the grace and instruction to do it. When that moment comes, sometimes it only takes me two days to create powerful digital art because it flows so smoothly. I have learned to completely depend on His flow, understanding that it will be produced because the Holy Spirit will help and guide me. There is such faith and peace knowing I can rest while I wait for His instructions. I don't need to fabricate something right away just to produce something.

   It is my prayer that we pray, seek His face and humble ourselves before Him to understand His divine instructions so we can become the extension of His eyes, ears, hands, and mind to create what He wants us to build for His glory.

2. **Test us** – God tests us so we can grow spiritually and eventually become completely developed in our faith, lacking in nothing as it was explained by James, "*Be assured that the testing of your faith [through experience] produces endurance [leading to spiritual maturity, and inner peace]. And let endurance have its perfect result*

and do a thorough work, so that you may be perfect and completely developed [in your faith], lacking in nothing" (James 1:3-4 AMP).

I believe I have come to a place where my creativity has gone to another level because of the experiences I had in the past that allowed me to be more dependent on God. I can say that my faith in Him to create arts that matter arose from times I have been tested to produce the need to wait on Him. However, I submit to you that I am still a canvas and a work of poetry in progress.

3. **Know what is in our heart** – There is a saying, "What's down in the well comes up in the bucket." Jesus said, *"For out of the abundance of the heart the mouth speaks"* (Matthew 12:34). We'll never know the deepest motivation of our hearts until we have trials or experiences that the Lord can use to show us what is truly in our hearts. That is why humility is crucial. We should never take our experiences and trials for granted. We must look at them as a way for the Lord to remove the callouses of our hearts and pull out the weeds of our lives, otherwise all the pains and emotions we have experienced will be for naught.

I remember being involved in projects that put us in debt and cost us hundreds of thousands of hard-earned dollars. It was excruciating, mainly because it involved trusted friends in the Body of Christ. However, one day I heard Him loud and clear in His still small voice, *Treat this experience as school fees for being in the School of the Holy Spirit.*

Wow! Something happened to me! I suddenly did not care about how much money we lost. All I could think of was that we had enrolled and paid top dollar to go to the best school possible to gain wisdom and increased discernment. They have risen to another level.

In the process, the Lord showed us the motivation of our hearts and the weeds that needed to go so we could make this upward move. We needed divine purging. It was a tremendous lesson in stewarding and multiplying God's finances correctly to help us navigate in the years ahead. I gladly share that as of this writing, we have paid our debts as well as their interest.

My prayer is for Jeremiah 17:10 to be activated in our lives, *"I, the Lord, search the heart, I test the mind, Even to give every man according to his ways, According to the fruit of his doings."*

Pray with me:

> *Do it now, Lord, search my heart and cleanse me of all the wrong motivations still in me that I may keep Your commandments.*

The end result is for the Lord to see whether we will keep His commandments or not. I'd rather be on the side of keeping His commandments, because it will guarantee us to be in the land He promised us to possess in Deuteronomy 8:6-9:

> Therefore you shall keep the commandments of the Lord your God, to walk in His ways and to fear Him. For the Lord your God is bringing you into a good land, a land of brooks of water, of fountains and springs, that flow out of valleys and hills; a land of wheat and barley, of vines and fig trees and pomegranates, honey; a land in which you will eat bread without scarcity, in which you will lack nothing; a land whose stones are iron and out of whose hills you can dig copper. When you have eaten and are full, then you shall bless the Lord your God for the good land which He has given you.

If we itemize the type of "land" the Lord wants us to possess, it enables us to recognize it when we see it. The knowledge that when we keep His commandments we are assured of arriving in our land of promise inspires us to do so. May we never miss ours! Here is the land we've been promised if we keep God's commandments:

- a good land
- a land of brooks of water
- a land of fountains and springs that flow out of valleys and hills
- a land of wheat and barley
- a land of vines, fig trees, and pomegranates
- a land of olive oil and honey
- a land where we will eat bread without scarcity
- a land where we will lack nothing
- a land whose stones are iron and out of whose hills you can dig copper

Deuteronomy 8:10 tells us why the Lord wants to give us this good land: it is for us to bless Him for the good land He gave us!

In the Old Testament when they say "remember the Lord," it is not merely a brain function of having an excellent memory to remember things. It is about remembering His covenant promises that are essential in creating wealth, because according to Deuteronomy 8:17-18,

> Otherwise, you may say in your heart, 'My power and the strength of my hand made me this wealth.' But you shall remember [with profound respect] the Lord your God, for it is He who is giving you power to make wealth, that He may confirm His covenant which He swore (solemnly promised) to your fathers, as it is this day.
>
> *(AMP)*

We must avoid the pitfall of verse 17: it is not by our own hand, nor our own power that we gain the wealth. We must remember that the Lord gives us the power to make, or create wealth for the sole purpose of fulfilling the covenant He promised our forefathers.

It is inevitable that when we begin to live in the creative realm, we will produce God-given ideas to make wealth, because He will give us the power to do it! We will be amiss if we fall in the pit of verse 17 to ever think that we did it out of our own ability and power. We must never forget what He has done, because our creativity will produce wealth. We must use that wealth to bless Him back!

As I was writing this, I sensed the Holy Spirit nudging me to write a prayer of repentance for not acknowledging God in this context, and to bring to the altar the wealth we have created if we haven't dedicated to Him.

> *In the mighty name of Jesus, I decree and declare Deuteronomy 8:17-18 over my life. I repent for not acknowledging You in the wealth that I have created through your inspired creative ideas. I dedicate and rededicate all the projects and creativity that You have bestowed on my life. I acknowledge that I have it because You have given it to me; I acknowledge that it was Your power that has given me the strength and supernatural ability to create, so I ask You to cleanse my hands for thinking otherwise. I ask You to bless my hands that they may be an extension of Yours from now on. Use them for Your glory! I beseech You to confirm the covenant that You have solemnly promised to our forefathers in Jesus' Mighty Name!*

Prayer of Release #12 – The Power to Create Wealth Through Creativity

Supernatural Decrees for Breakthrough

The Word says in Job 22:28, "decree a thing and it shall be established," therefore,

- I decree and declare Deuteronomy 8:18 over my life: *"And you shall remember the Lord your God, for it is He who gives you power to get wealth, that He may establish His covenant which He swore to your fathers, as it is this day."* I will never forget that God gives me the power to create wealth so He can establish His covenant with my generation.

- I decree and declare the Lord has my permission to search my heart and cleanse me of all the wrong motivations so that I can keep His commandments.

- I decree and declare that I keep the commandments of the Lord my God to walk in His ways and to fear Him. The fear of the Lord is upon me as a restraining order for any wrong motivations that may try to creep into my walk.

- I decree and declare that I follow and obey every commandment God has commanded me today. I am careful to observe them that I may live and multiply and go in and possess the land that the Lord swore to my forefathers.

- I decree and declare that I possess the land that He commanded me to occupy. I have the discernment to know which land to possess. As I inhabit the land I increase in my fruitfulness in the land. It is a land of abundance.

Life Application Section

Memory Verse

And you shall remember the Lord your God, for it is He who gives you power to get wealth, that He may establish His covenant which He swore to your fathers, as it is this day. *(Deuteronomy 8:18)*

Reflections

1. Why is it important to remember the Lord?
   _____
   _____
   _____
   _____
   _____

2. What is the pitfall of Deuteronomy 8:17? Why should we avoid it?
   _____
   _____
   _____
   _____
   _____

CHAPTER 13

CREATIVITY AND PERSONALITY

> For with God, nothing will be impossible.
>
> *(Luke 1:37)*

> For since the creation of the world His invisible attributes are clearly seen, being understood by the things that are made, even His eternal power and Godhead, so that they are without excuse,
>
> *(Romans 1:20)*

> Every new idea is an impossibility until it is born.
>
> *(Ron Brown)*

When speaking of God, Paul was clear in Romans 1:20, *"For since the creation of the world His invisible attributes are clearly seen, being understood by the things that are made, even His eternal power and Godhead, so that they are without excuse,"* His invisible attributes and divine nature are clearly seen, which means that His characteristics, qualities, and intrinsic value become visible through what He has made and created. We are His creation, therefore His invisible creative attributes must be seen through us!

In this chapter I would like to touch on different personalities and characteristics of creativity. I believe that these areas affect the way we create. My purpose is for us to better understand our personality and how we process our thoughts and creative ideas so we can become better in our creative process. This understanding will give us a resolve to be more intentional in ensuring that God's creative attributes are seen and understood throughout our lives.

What are the characteristics of a creative mind?

Creative people have a particular process they use when they plan, create, implement and maintain what they have chosen to produce or do. The first five characteristics are based on Dr. Robert Muller's study, but I have used my definition and description and applied it to how to live in the creative realm.

1. *A positive attitude* – I once heard the story of a wise old man who sat at the border of a town. A man passing by asked the old man, "How is this place? I heard that this place is not safe and that there are robbers that attack at night." The old man replied, "You are right."

    Another man came and asked, "How is this place? I heard that there are amazing opportunities to start a business here." The old man replied, "You are right!"

    The old man's answers were a reflection of the attitude of the person asking the question: one's attitude was negative, the other's was positive. Both received what they expect.

    Creative people always see the glass as half full instead of half empty. We can create a positive environment and choose to prosper in it, or a negative environment and die suppressed and depressed in it.

    Most creative people have a positive outlook on life and do not allow an obstruction in their journey to deter them from stepping to the side of the road until the obstruction is gone.

They tackle their task from the perspective of crossing the finish line no matter who is behind or ahead of them.

2. *Fearlessness* – I have a whole chapter on fear, but fearlessness is one of the characteristics of creativity that is very hard to deny. Fear is the consciousness of possible danger, or upcoming unpleasant circumstances.

   When we first moved to Arizona, we stayed with a beautiful couple before we moved to our place. A particular part of the neighborhood was unsafe, but I did not know. I went to a vegetable and fruit store that had inexpensive farm-to-table produce at least once a week. Then one day, one of our friends found out that I went to that store and told me how brave I was going there alone. I was not afraid because I was unaware the place was unsafe. Even after I was told, I didn't allow that fear to affect me, and I continued shopping there until we moved.

   People have aborted their creativity because of the paralyzing effect of a fear they have allowed to invade their temple. The fearless ones, however, can be spotted from afar because of how they proceed with their journey.

   I encourage you, *fear not* and develop a life of fearlessness by trusting in the Lord. Create without fear!

3. *Strong motivation and determination* – Daniel, our nephew from Zambia, Africa, is very good at computers and was accepted at a Christian college in Tennessee. I am proud of his unusual motivation and determination to succeed. He texted me saying when he arrives here in the US, he will fast for three days and nights "because America is different." He needed to seek God to possess the land.

   Creative people are motivated and determined to be successful. They will not allow hindrances to prevent them from pursuing their vision. Laziness is not their portion, but passion is their constant companion!

4. *Flexibility* – Flexibility is the ability to bend easily without breaking. I believe it is one of the antidotes to change, because according to *Merriam-Webster Dictionary*, flexibility is "characterized by a ready capability to adapt to new, different, or changing requirements."

   Creative people are flexible. They can easily adapt to the environment and tasks set before them. They don't limit their productivity to one idea and strategy.

   Have you been with people who see everything as black and white? There is no flexibility and room to adjust based on what is presented to them. They get frazzled and anxious as soon as they are faced with unfamiliar tasks or situations. These people are not flexible about moving to another location, changing jobs, and often have difficulty adapting to new company policies.

   One last thought on this topic.

   I believe that if we allow God to operate in our creativity, flexibility will naturally come with it.

5. *Intense curiosity* – Sir Ken Robinson once said, "You can't just give someone a creativity injection. You have to create an environment for curiosity and a way to encourage people and get the best out of them." *Commonsensemedia.org* defines curiosity as a strong desire to know or learn something. Creative people who have this characteristic are not afraid to ask questions to get the information they need to create. They know how to listen so they can learn more. I am always amazed at some people who want to meet my husband Francis because of the books he has written, but when we get a chance to spend time with them, they do all the talking about themselves and don't allow Francis to

share more of the revelation and wisdom God has imparted to him.

Intense curiosity is a trait that drove Albert Einstein's creativity. He said, "I have no special talents. I am only passionately curious….The important thing is not to stop questioning. Curiosity has its own reason for existing."

6. *Originality* – Originality is the ability to be innovative by producing creative ideas and things that have not been seen or heard before. Originality truly manifests the unseen into the seen by pulling a concept from the creative realm and producing it in the material, or natural realm.

7. *Open mindedness* – According to *Merriam-Webster Dictionary*, an open mind is "the willingness to listen to or accept different ideas or opinions." This is a characteristic of a creative person who does not fear their ideas being challenged. They are not persuaded by what they hear and see or by others' opinions. They keep an open mind and don't shy away from new ideas, but are willing to understand, discover, and experiment to reach their desired outcome.

8. *Risk taking* – Risk takers are not afraid to take a chance, or try to get to the next level. Risk takers are willing to go to unchartered territory, that could also be dangerous, to seek opportunities for increase, growth, and achieving the desired goal.

Harriet Tubman was born into slavery in Maryland around 1820 but escaped to the North in 1849. Tubman used a complex system of safe houses called the Underground Railroad as a trail to freedom and later decided to help other slaves escape the same way. She made 19 trips from the South from 1850 to 1860, guiding more than 300 slaves to freedom.

It certainly took a creative mind to create the underground railroad. What would have happened to the slaves who escaped because of her efforts if she had not taken that risk?

9. *Problem solving* – Problem solvers are creative people who will not stop until they find the solution to the problem they are trying to solve. They are those who become a solution to a purpose that needs to be fulfilled. Their focus and determination to succeed supersedes any notion that the task might be impossible. Their only impossibility is that the possible has not yet been achieved. The primary reason why Thomas Edison successfully invented the light bulb was that he did not stop at the first step. He continued until he discovered the solution.

10. *Continuously learning and experimenting* – Creative people are constantly learning and experimenting. They pursue education to master their trade and further advance their skills.

    Jeriel is our webmaster and part of our media team. I have seen him improve throughout the years of working with them. Why do I mention that? Jeriel graduated in nursing, and most of his technological and creative skills are self-taught through e-courses and free online teachings. If he can do it, we can also be successful in honing and improving our skills to be more creative.

11. *Practice Zero-Based Thinking* – Creative people practice Zero-Based Thinking. This is an excellent decision/thinking technique developed by Brian Tracy. Zero-based thinkers continually ask themselves, *If I wasn't now doing what I am doing, knowing what I now know, would I start?* If the answer is no, they cut their losses, discontinue what they are doing and do something else.

Zero-based thinking gives us the rare opportunity to ask ourselves if there is anything in our lives we should do more of, less of, start or stop. Zero-based thinking is the ability to stop a project if it is not working. Are you willing to stop doing something in which you've invested a lot of time and energy if it is no longer working?

12. *Eliminate their ego* – This is a quality of creative thinkers. They are more concerned about what's right than who's right. Their pride doesn't get in the way because their goal is to get the job done rather than pacify the one getting it done. They are more open to accepting other's ideas, concepts, and methods to attain their desired outcome. Some of my paintings were perfected during their creation process because of someone's input. I remember when I was creating one of my pieces called *The Victor's Crown*. I was putting the roaring lion on the side of the wooden cross when Francis recommended for me to put it in the middle of the wooden cross (see the picture in Chapter 13: My Creative Journey). As soon as I moved it, the painting became more powerful! It is actually one of my most popular pieces.

13. *No to entitlement* – Creative thinkers do not have an entitlement mentality. The Lord gave me the meaning and understanding of what entitlement mentality is. It is a mindset of believing one deserves to partake of someone's success, money and property without asking for permission. They assume that they can just eat from someone's hard earned platter without working for it. They love handouts without the corresponding merit or work to earn it. This type of person prevents their creativity from flowing because they depend on another person's creativity or productivity, so they fail to tend to, or activate theirs.

Creative thinkers are of the complete opposite mind. They are always activating their creativity. Their dependency is on the creative ideas produced through communion with the Spirit of Creativity, not from the creative ideas of others whom they can milk without investing their own time, energy and proper contribution. They are not manipulators or connivers, and don't steal. They work hard to create and produce what was assigned to them.

The creative process

The creative process involves stages from the inception of a thought or creative idea to its manifestation through a progression of thoughts and actions. It requires problem-solving and critical thinking skills – the kind of thinking in which you question, analyze, interpret, and evaluate an issue to form a judgment. It is aimed at achieving the best possible outcomes in any situation.

1. **Preparation** – *Idea Generation Phase*
   This is the stage when we start to get ideas. Much research and gathering of information is done in this stage. Here we also brainstorm, write our ideas down and consider the different approaches we can use to build our ideas.

2. **Incubation** – *Development Phase*
   At this stage all the information and research we have gathered starts to churn and blend together. There is no time frame on this. It could take days, weeks, months, or even years. In this stage, we continually seek God to add to layers of creative ideas He has given us, and we meditate to get more clarity on how to proceed with the idea.

3. **Insight** – *The Aha Moment Phase*
   Your "Eureka" or "AHA" moment is when everything suddenly clicks. The light bulb finally turns on, and we see the

big picture. At this stage we gain deeper understanding of our idea. It could also be a sudden understanding of a complicated or complex problem we have been trying to solve. We can now perceive clearly after we have incubated and marinated the idea.

4. **Evaluation** – *Assessment Phase*
   This phase is crucial because here we determine whether the idea will work or not before we waste more time and energy. I must say that not all creative ideas are worth pursuing. Evaluation is the stage where our ego is tested to see if we should drop what we have been incubating all this time. We must evaluate whether the idea is genuinely from the Lord, and if we are in His proper timing. Allowing others to give us feedback is helpful at this stage. This vital input ensures that the idea is worth bringing to the next stage of creative development.

5. **Verification** – *The Phase of Manifestation*
   At this final stage we find ourselves doing the work. The innovative product might be a song, an architectural design, a formula made up of natural herbs to fight cancer, a clothing line, or anything propelled by the initial stage of the creative process. This is where we finalize our idea to bring it to life to fulfill the purpose God has ordained for us in our Book of Destiny.

Types of thinking as applied to creativity and problem solving

Convergent thinking – Convergent thinking focuses on reaching one well-defined solution to a problem. This type of thinking is best suited for tasks involving logic instead of creativity, such as answering multiple-choice tests, or solving a problem where you know there are no other possible solutions.

Convergent thinking is also known as critical, vertical, analytical, or linear thinking. It pulls together all known facts and examines them logically to find the best final answer. The main goal of convergent thinking is finding a single, probable solution to any problem. This mode of thinking emphasizes speed, logic, and accuracy.[12]

Characteristics of convergent thinkers

- Fast – Convergent thinkers focus on moving quickly because they aim to find the best direct solution most efficiently in a shorter time.
- Precise – They arrive at an accurate answer after the process is completed.
- Logical – They apply reasoning clearly and consistently.
- Methodical – They commonly use a linear method and rational steps to find the correct solution.

Divergent thinking

Divergent thinking is the opposite of convergent thinking and involves more creativity. With this type of thinking you can generate ideas most people don't think about, develop multiple solutions and ways to deal with a problem and improve on existing ideas. This method usually produces innovative solutions to a pressing problem. Divergent thinkers are often risk takers, curious, flexible, and independent. While divergent thinking often involves brainstorming for many possible answers to a question, the goal is the same as for convergent thinking—to arrive at the best solution.

Characteristics of divergent thinkers

- Instinctive – Ideas are highly spontaneous, usually prompted by instinct and arising from impulse or a natural inclination.

- Free-Flowing – Ideas keep coming. Even though the answer has already been found, other possibilities or answers are still considered.
- Complex – Concepts are multilayered and involve numerous points of view.

Both Divergent and Convergent thinking methods are vital in our lives. Neither is better or superior to the other. When faced with a problem that needs our creative solutions, we look at different possibilities (divergence) and then narrow them down to get the best solution (convergence).

We can use both divergent and convergent thinking for creative problem solving as follows:

1. *Discover* – The first step of creative problem solving is discovery. Here we use divergent thinking. When we encounter problems, we look at the root cause by considering all possibilities to arrive at the best possible solution.

    A social media director could have a problem with why their subscribers are decreasing instead of having steady growth. The divergent thinker will consider all possibilities for the decrease, including the demographics, target advertising, the time their content was posted, topics that were shared, the different types of content, and the consistency of their posts. They would analyze the various statistics to understand better the possible cause of subscriber decline.

2. *Define* – This second stage uses convergent thinking to find the solution to the problem. Perhaps limited advertising caused the decline of subscribers, but if the problem arose due to irrelevant content, then the focus would be on posting content more relevant to readers.

3. *Deduce* – This third stage requires divergent thinking to find possible solutions that help the company be more current and relevant in its content. Some possible solutions could include more thorough research of relevant topics, understanding the behavior of subscribers, hiring a consulting company to provide analysis regarding followers, and increasing the advertising budget.

4. *Determine* – In this final problem-solving stage, we must go back to convergent thinking to find the best solution for eliminating the problem. While all the possible solutions are reasonable in Stage 3, here we start with one action to implement. In certain instances, we might focus on more than one solution, but we must be mindful only to pursue those most closely related to the issue. In our example, the social media director might hire a third-party company specializing in market analysis to help understand the behavioral pattern of their subscribers and include target advertising to increase their subscriber base.

I pray this chapter helps us gain more insight into the way we process ideas. My goal has been to provide you with information and research on ways to enhance your understanding of how our personality, creative characteristics, and thinking styles impact our creativity.

We can continually develop our creativity and the ways we process ideas.

Take the first step.

Don't allow discouragement to hinder you.

Just believe!

Always remember: the Spirit of Creativity lives inside you, and it is up to you to make the right choice, take that step and start living in the creative realm.

Father, I decree and declare that my creative ability is increased and enhanced, and Your nature and attributes can be clearly seen in my life. May I be the visible representation of Your invisible attributes so You will be understood through my life. Lord, help me discover the creative skills I have not tapped into so I can fully manifest what You have given me in Jesus' Mighty Name!

PRAYER OF RELEASE #13
– CREATIVITY AND PERSONALITY

Supernatural Decrees for Breakthrough

The Word says in Job 22:28, "decree a thing and it shall be established," therefore,

- I decree and declare that I am the visible representation of the invisible God. The world will understand God's eternal power and divine nature through me. Everything I do represents Him. My life allows others to discover God's invisible qualities through me.

- I decree and declare discouragement does hinder me. I believe! I always remember that the Spirit of Creativity is living inside of me. I make the necessary choices to start living in the creative realm.

- I decree and declare that I am a creative thinker more concerned about what's right than who is right. My pride and my ego do not hinder my ability to work with others to get the job done. I am accepting of other's ideas, concepts and methods to attain God's desired outcome.

- I decree and declare that I have insight into my personality and the way I process thoughts and creative ideas. I am resolved to be more intentional in making sure that God's creative attributes are seen and understood through my life.

- I decree and declare that I have an open mind in the way I create. I do not get offended when my ideas are challenged. I am not persuaded by what I see and hear, or by opinions of others. I have an open mind and don't shy away from new ideas. I am willing to understand, discover, and experiment to reach God's desired outcome.

LIFE APPLICATION SECTION

Memory Verse

For since the creation of the world His invisible attributes are clearly seen, being understood by the things that are made, even His eternal power and Godhead, so that they are without excuse. *(Romans 1:20)*

Reflections

1. What is the difference between Divergent Thinking and Convergent Thinking?
   _____
   _____
   _____
   _____
   _____

2. What creative characteristics do you have?
   _____
   _____
   _____
   _____
   _____

CHAPTER 14

MY CREATIVE JOURNEY

> I will praise you to all my brothers; I will stand up before the congregation and testify of the wonderful things you have done.
>
> *(Psalm 22:22)*

> Your story is the key that can unlock someone else's prison.
>
> *(Unknown Author)*

I have been creative since I was a child. An "A" grade was typical for me, especially in the Arts, from kindergarten to college. However, I must admit that my creativity went to another level when I came to the Lord. My artistic ability to create digital arts started when I worked as a volunteer for a pastor in Long Island. She is a prophetic writer, and I offered to create her newsletter. However, I got frustrated when I couldn't find pictures to portray some of her prophetic dreams, and if I found one, it was subject to copyright. This frustration led me to learn Photoshop, a graphic design software program, not knowing the Lord was using my frustration to get me to learn digital arts because He knew it was part of His plan for me.

I've been asked many times how I do it. I can honestly say it's through divine inspiration that comes in different ways. I believe we have a library of creative ideas in Heaven written on a scroll. It requires great determination to have communion with the Holy Spirit and seek the wisdom of God so we can access our library in Heaven and read the scrolls that contain the creative ideas He has assigned for us. But nothing happens if we don't get out of our comfort zone so we can enter heaven's library to find the scroll we need to access.

Learning is important as well. I cannot stress enough the importance of learning our trade, or art so that when grace and revelation come, we are ready to bring it into its manifestation on earth.

In this chapter I am including pictures of some of my prophetic paintings and explanations how I got the creative ideas. I hope you enjoy the digital arts I have chosen even though it is in black and white.

Intercessors Arise

This piece was birthed when I learned that the Suzanne Hinn National Prayer planned to have an Intercessors' Conference. The inspiration to create a piece for their conference theme came immediately.

I knew I would create a painting with Queen Esther as the main focus. The Lord used her as a deliverer to win freedom for the Jewish Nation from the wrath of Haman through her intercession.

I created a picture of Queen Esther holding a Bible to indicate that intercessors need the Word to pray through their petitions. It is a must to declare the Word to call into being those things that are not.

I then added the map of America because the Suzanne Hinn National Prayer call has been called to pray for America. I included the scepter to represent the favor that was granted to her by the King when he extended it toward her and said, *"What do you wish, Queen Esther? What is your request? It shall be given to you—up to half the kingdom!"*

The dove is present in most of my paintings to represent the Holy Spirit – who is the Spirit of Creativity. I included the clock to represent the epoch of time Esther was in when Mordecai said, *"For if you remain silent at this time, relief and deliverance for the Jews will arise from another place, but you and your father's family will perish. And who knows but that you have come to your royal position for such a time as this?"* (Esther 4:14)

I chose the background of a throne and crown representing our kingly and governmental anointing to influence kings in the marketplace and in our government.

My Creative Journey

Divine Restraining Order from the Courts of Heaven

My husband released a book called *Issuing Divine Restraining Orders from the Courts of Heaven*. Sid Roth interviewed him on, *It's Supernatural* and the show had an overwhelming response. We were amazed at the breakthrough and healing that came from that teaching. I was in prayer when the idea came to me to create artwork to complement his teaching. This piece was birthed.

This artwork shows someone with his hand raised indicating his desire to go before the Courts of Heaven and petition the court to issue a divine restraining order against his accuser. It depicts victory won against his adversary in the Courts of Heaven.

I have included a statement that he has been granted a restraining order from the highest court and the primary Scripture concerning the Courts of Heaven in Daniel 7:9-10.

To indicate a courtroom, I used the gavel as a focal point. I included the Bible to represent our Book of Destiny since we go to the Courts of Heaven to petition the court against the enemy's scheme to keep us from knowing our purpose recorded in our Book of Destiny.

I also like to put little extra touches in my paintings. Notice the ancient plume on the scroll and the scale to represent the courtroom.

The Key to Unlocking your Destiny

When I was creating this piece, I had nothing in mind except the background. As soon as the background was in place, all the ideas and symbolism I needed to put into the artwork came forth. In this case I had to take the first step and allow the Holy Spirit to instruct me as I started to create.

The tree in the middle represents Yeshua, the Tree of Life. The key represents the truth that abiding in the Word is the key to unlocking our destiny based on John 15:7: *"If you abide in Me, and My words abide in you, you will ask what you desire, and it shall be done for you."*

I showed a man's silhouette on the Bible as the dove (the Holy Spirit) rises out of him. I wanted to convey here that we need both the Spirit and the Word if we are to unlock our destiny.

The Lion and the Lamb

This artwork was inspired by the Book of Revelation:

> And I saw in the right hand of Him who sat on the throne a scroll written inside and on the back, sealed with seven seals. Then I saw a strong angel proclaiming with a loud voice, "Who is worthy to open the scroll and to loose its seals?" And no one in heaven or on the earth or under the earth was able to open the scroll, or to look at it.
>
> So I wept much, because no one was found worthy to open and read the scroll, or to look at it. But one of the elders said to me, "Do not weep. Behold, the Lion of the tribe of Judah, the

Root of David, has prevailed to open the scroll and to loose its seven seals.

> And I looked, and behold, in the midst of the throne and of the four living creatures, and in the midst of the elders, stood a Lamb as though it had been slain, having seven horns and seven eyes, which are the seven Spirits of God sent out into all the earth. Then He came and took the scroll out of the right hand of Him who sat on the throne.
>
> *(Revelation 5:1-7)*

I meditated on this passage of the Bible and came up with the artwork. The scroll points to the One worthy to open the scroll. The Lion represents Jesus as the Lion of the Tribe of Judah, who is the One worthy of opening the scroll. I included the Lamb with seven horns and seven eyes, which are the seven Spirits of God sent out into all the earth.

My Creative Journey

The Victor's Crown

The Victor's Crown was birthed through the help of my husband. I found a picture of a wooden cross and had the idea of putting near it a lion that represented the Lion of Judah roaring to release His deliverance. When I was working on this piece, I originally put the roaring lion on the side, but it wasn't working. I knew something was missing, and did not feel the anointing, or release to finalize it. When I showed it to my husband, he suggested I put it in the middle of the cross. Everything clicked as soon as I moved it, and I felt the peace and anointing because it symbolizes Jesus on the Cross, His death was as the Lamb, but the roaring Lion of Judah is the conqueror who wears the victor's crown.

Sometimes the Scripture comes after I finish my piece. That happened in this case. After I finished it, the Lord gave me Revelation 6:1-2,

> Now I saw when the Lamb opened one of the seals; and I heard one of the four living creatures saying with a voice like thunder, "Come and see." And I looked, and behold, a white horse. He who sat on it had a bow; and a crown was given to him, and he went out conquering and to conquer.

Nashville

Nashville is home to some of the world's most famous and respected music venues. Many music artists, past and present, call Music City home. One day I thought of honoring our Nashville friends through my artwork. That is how this piece was birthed.

In this painting you see instruments, musical symbols, and silhouettes of musicians playing their instruments. I have included some of Nashville's famous buildings and structures.

We have become very good friends with Jozef Nuyens and his wife Lana, owner of *Castle Recordings Studio*, which has recorded 500 gold and platinum albums of musicians from Bon Jovi to Michael W. Smith. I asked his permission if I could use his logo that I put on the big guitar to honor him. I then finalized it with additional details representing the Kingdom, like the cross on the harmonica and the lion on the percussion drum.

The Eighth Mountain - The Mountain of God

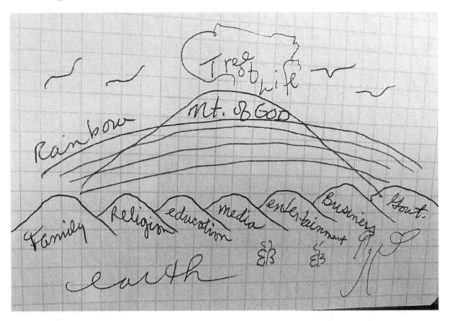

Lastly I want to share a piece I finished at the time of this writing called, *The Eighth Mountain – The Mountain of God.*

This design is a perfect example of how the grace of God came flawlessly to create what is in the Mind of God.

I got a phone call from Dr. Alveda King at the time when I was finalizing this book and assisting my husband in a conference where he was the main speaker. I was swamped. Alveda asked me if I could create a piece for her to depict the Eighth Mountain which is the Mountain of God and the Seven Mountains of Influence based on the teaching by Dr. Lance Walnau. The teaching states that there are Seven Mountains of Influence over which, as believers, we should be exercising dominion and the authority God has given us. You can see these mountains of Influence in the artwork.

Alveda sent me a draft of how she envisioned the design to be portrayed. What is amazing is that grace immediately came despite my busy schedule. The spirit of acceleration came upon me, and I finished it in no time. I added a few symbols to her original ideas, i.e., the Scripture, lion, and the angels.

I am very encouraged to use my artwork and its process of creation to let you see how I access the creative realm. I desire for all of His children to realize they are born creative and have the ability to create in them. I pray this book gives you good insight into your creativity and ignites the passion and desire that has always been in you. May your life manifest the creativity that God has given you!

Please don't hesitate to share a praise report how this book has unleashed your potential to create and bring forth what was in God's mind for you to do before you were born so you can advance His Kingdom.

Your creativity is one of your tools for warfare

Many people don't realize that our creativity is a tool of warfare. An author fights the enemy through his/her books that communicate revelation to readers. This revelation changes readers' mindsets enabling them to combat demonic doctrines and to realign with the principles and culture of God's Kingdom.

A choreographer's tool is their creative ability to compose an anointed dance depicting the unseen so that when people watch they see what is hidden and healing occurs.

A clothing designer creates outfits that bring glory to the Lord among unbelievers. The designs can be so anointed that unbelievers can't help but strike up a conversation that allows the message of the Kingdom to be shared.

Now that you have taken your precious time to read this book, I pray that you get a more profound revelation of your creative nature and ability through your communion with the Holy Spirit, the Spirit of Creativity.

> *I decree and declare that your untapped potential is unleashed, and you discover your divine design recorded in your Book of Destiny.*
>
> *I decree and declare that you discover innate wisdom hidden in God for your glory.*
>
> *I pray that His intrinsic value in you will be seen so that the kingdom of this world becomes the Kingdom of our God!*
>
> *I honor your gift, and I celebrate your purpose and destiny.*

Let's come together to bring forth and release God's creativity here on earth, in the mighty name of Jesus!

> Remember, you are unique – fearfully, and wonderfully made. You are a walking poem – a piece of art; a masterpiece created by the Master Craftsman.
>
> *(Carmela Myles)*

Endnotes

Chapter 1
1. https://www.indeed.com/career-advice/career-development/creativity-and-innovation-examples

Chapter 3
2. https://www.biblestudytools.com/lexicons/greek/nas/parakletos.html

Chapter 5
3. https://www.thegospelcoalition.org/article/jesus-proverbs/

Chapter 7
4. https://www.masterclass.com/articles/poetry-101-what-is-a-stanza-in-poetry-stanza-definition-with-examples#what-is-a-stanza-in-poetry

5. https://www.liveabout.com/mary-lou-retton-3529897

Chapter 9
6. https://www.insidermonkey.com/blog/16-accidental-scientific-discoveries-and-inventions-made-by-mistake-652059/?singlepage=1

Chapter 10
7. https://www.productplan.com/glossary/eisenhower-matrix/

Chapter 11
8. https://www.huffpost.com/entry/exercise-creativity-physical-activity_n_4394310#:~:text=Regular%20Exercise%20Could%20Boost%20Creativity.%20Specifically%2C%20researchers%20noted,for%20one%20problem%2C%20while%20the%20latter%20involves%20thinking

9. https://www.independent.co.uk/life-style/health-and-families/wang-deshun-80-year-old-chinese-runway-model-fitness-regime-gym-health-youth-swimming-skates-a7654231.html

10. Aarp.org/health

Chapter 12
11. https://www.pbs.org/wnet/civilization-west-and-rest/killer-apps/property/discussion-what-is-the-importance-of-land-ownership-today/

Chapter 13
12. https://www.indeed.com/career-advice/career-development/convergent-thinking

Made in the USA
Middletown, DE
25 October 2022